Transforming Culture:
The Church at Work
in the World

By:
Gerald H. Twombly, President
Development Marketing
Associates, Inc.

Phone toll-free: 1-866-DMA-FIRST
http://www.developmentmarketing.com

ISBN: 0-9748144-0-7

Cover design by SPC Design and Printing, Syracuse, Indiana

Printed in U.S.A. by
Evangel Press
Nappanee, Indiana

Dedication

To three whose lives
have impacted mine:

To Lynda Shelhamer, a Godly nurse

To Bill Chapman, a physcian who
reflects the character of
God in his work and life

To Tom Streeter, my pastor, who has been
wonderfully used of God to train
and equip the church for the joy of ministry

Table of Contents

Preface 7

Introduction 11

1. The Assignment 15

2. A Nurse Who Changed 21

3. The Pastor 27

4. A Relationship Restored 35

5. Community Church 41

6. Relationships 49

7. Incomplete by Design 55

8. The Vision 61

9. Critical Groups 67

10. A Church At Work 75

11. Outreach 83

12. A Church Triumphant 91

The Conclusion 95

Appendices 97

Transforming Your Culture Covenant 111

Preface

This is a book about the church.

I cannot remember a time when church wasn't a part of my life. My earliest memories of growing up seem to revolve around church. I have images of my grandmother playing a pump organ in a country church, of her singing louder than anyone else in the congregation, of covered dish dinners, laughter, and men throwing horseshoes at church picnics.

But much of church to me was irrelevant. While I can track many of the relationships I treasure in life back to church, much of what I remember was that church was perfunctory. Church was something "good Christians" did and while my value system was impacted by what I experienced, there was a sense in which I felt left out and not an integral part of what it was that happened there.

This is a book about change.

For all the apprehension I have experienced over the years with church, I have earnestly loved the church and have strongly believed that God planted His Church in the world to be the organism through which the glorious message of the redemption He has offered to all through the work of Christ.

"Redemption not only generates life, it generates change!"

But for all its potential, it has seemed to me that the church is bogged down with incidentals and has missed the main point in terms of its purpose. Redemption not only generates life, it generates change. And it seems that if meaningful change and true revival is to occur in the world in which we live, the primary facilitator must be the church, the local church that is strategically planted in communities around the world.

This is a book about relationships.

I have come to believe that the kind of change that God wants to accomplish in people and in society will occur most effectively in the context of relationships. It is through relationships that we grow individually in our love relationship with Christ and it will be through relationship that we will reach our world with the message of forgiveness that is available through Christ's completed work on Calvary.

This is a book about time and opportunity.

The older I become, the more I am reminded of the words of James: "Life is but a vapour which soon cometh and then passes away."[1] God has granted us a tiny bit of time in which to impact those things that really count for eternity. I believe we live in a world that in its selfish pursuits has lost its focus and has come woefully short in finding answers to life's most perplexing issues. For those of us who have found answers in a personal and intimate relationship with Christ, these are days of unparalleled opportunity. I believe the "fields (of our time) are certainly ripe to harvest"[2] and it is up to us to exercise our responsibilities in bearing the message of Christ's love and the redemptive work He has accomplished on our behalf. Bearing that message is the essence of this book and, it seems to me, a most worthy pursuit.

Grappling with the brevity of life caused me to write this poem, a woefully inadequate expression of those things God has impressed upon me:

I walked one day
A long, long way
And came across an open space
The dead we buried in that place.

1. James 4:14
2. John 4:35

Before me was a granite stone,
Off by itself, it stood alone,
And on that stone there was a name,
Two dates, a dash, it was the same

As many other stones around
There alone upon a mound.
A date for birth, a date for death
The simple dash was only left.

A life, I thought, has now gone by,
The days I'm sure all seemed to fly,
And now a dash is left to say
This life has past, not one more day.

Some days seemed long, and others short,
We bank them all, not one abort,
And then comes one, like all that past,
When God says now, this is your last.

And then alone, before God lay,
Not many words were had to say,
"Here is my life. The work I've done,
Here's all I did, this is the sum."

I wonder what did happen next,
As God stood there, His gaze on him fixed?
What words were said to Him who lay,
Upon the ground, no more to say?

Life's challenges over, the time has past
Our work is done but what will last?
Some are ashes, others gold,
Those done in faith will not grow old.

I thought while looking on that stone,
The name, the dates, the dash that shown,
What impact will my work, the sum,
Will eternity be richer when my life is done?

This is a book about organization.

I did not intend to write a book about theology. What I have sought to accomplish is to write a book that could serve as a manual for organizations committed to facilitating change in their world.

US News and World Report recently reported that 40% of all Americans identify themselves as "evangelical Christians." It seems that we don't lack the personnel resources to make a decided difference in our world. God has planted His church everywhere; we certainly don't lack the organism through which this work could be accomplished. The redemptive message of the gospel of Jesus Christ can change lives, we don't lack a life-changing story to tell. What appears to be lacking is passion, a strategic plan, and a practical and functional organizational structure to help us achieve what "salt and light" are intended to accomplish—a significant impact on the culture of our respective worlds.

I am grateful to many people who have encouraged me in this project. Scores around the world have read versions of the manuscript and a dear friend, Lynelle Knight, was gracious enough to carefully edit my work. To those readers, spiritual mentors, and professional supporters I extend my deepest thanks.

The story told in this book is fictitious as is the church and the characters. The people, however, bear the names of three people who have had a significant impact on my life and who fulfill professional roles similar to those described in the book. While they have personality traits like those I describe, the activities depicted in the book come from my imagination.

There can yet be worldwide revival and it is my sincere prayer that God might graciously grant this book a reception among His church and that collectively local churches around the world might catch the vision it seeks to share and that change will begin, at first in communities and cities, and then spread like a huge fire across countries and continents and that millions might come to faith in Christ and that we, my generation, might impact our world for the eternal glory of God.

Gerald H. Twombly, 2004

Introduction

He worked at a local newspaper.

A feature writer of some renown, the Journalist penned stories that stirred the hearts of readers. His assignments took him into difficult places and required him to ask difficult questions. He sought to uncover the underlying issues that impact a culture shaped by the life experiences of those who influence it.

As time passed he found himself becoming all the things he disdained. Journalistic investigation brought to light many unsavory aspects of society that he wanted to deny even existed. Too many stories on addiction, homelessness, prison reform, and political and corporate corruption had taken a heavy personal toll on him.

The impact on his attitude became as unsavory to him as the stories he was assigned to research.

" . . . the inner struggle to reconcile his growing cynicism with the endless needs of society led to an almost palpable despair."

Looking back, he could clearly see a progression, first evidenced by discouragement. "How could a society as enlightened as ours permit these bad things to happen?" he wondered.

Discouragement led to frustration, which he was quick to express in the feature stories he wrote. He simply couldn't understand why people could look the other way in full view of the travesties he reported.

He thought he could deal with the discouragement, but as time passed the Journalist found himself retreating into apathy. An assignment to expose financial mismanagement by a local corporation elicited little more than a shrug. "I'll do it for whatever difference it will make," he remarked to his editor. As soon as he mouthed the words, he became aware of his apathy – that subtle step from frustration that eventually leads to cynicism.

He wrote the story about financial mismanagement and scores of others in the ensuing years. As his professional stock was rising, the inner struggle to reconcile his growing cynicism with the endless needs of the society led to an almost palpable despair.

It was at this point he got the assignment.

Think About It . . .

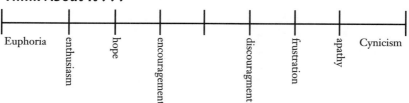

1. The line above is called "The Attitude Continuum." Everyone is somewhere between euphoria and cynicism on this imaginary line. In the case of The Journalist, he found himself becoming cynical about his profession and could track the steps that took him there. In relationship to this same line, place dots that reflect your attitudes towards the following relationships:

    A. Your Job
    B. Your Church
    C. The Relationship with Your Spouse

2. Write down some of the reasons why you placed yourself where you did on the continuum.

3. Think about it.

Chapter One

The Assignment

It was a sunny morning, one of those crisp autumn days when life seems almost perfect. The temperature was in the low 70s and the humidity had dropped significantly from those intolerable "dog days of summer."

Although it was the setting for a perfect day, life couldn't have been worse. The Journalist made the mistake of reading his e-mail the moment he woke up and was immediately intrigued by this memo note: "A critical response to your article." While not an uncommon introduction to the missives he regularly received from readers, this one happened to be from the mayor.

Double clicking on the icon produced a disturbing letter. It began, "I typically enjoy your articles and investigative reporting. You have a great talent of making the mundane interesting and capturing the attention of your readers."

"Life is a sick game mismanaged by a bureaucracy of self-proclaimed experts indifferent to anything that doesn't match their agenda."

Had it ended there it might have been a better day. But the letter went on, ". . . what is disturbing to me is how you use your position of influence. Your recent article on the plight of the poor of our city brought to light some interesting concerns but made recommendations in direct opposition to clearly stated positions city government has taken on the subject of urban renewal." From there it only got worse with questions of loyalty raised, "bigger issues" that were ignored, and several references to his personal irresponsibility and that of his newspaper.

A copy of the correspondence was sent to his editor along

with a demand for a follow-up article giving "a more balanced perspective" or the resignation of the Journalist.

The Journalist stared for a long time at the communiqué, chest heaving. "Life is a sick game mismanaged by a bureaucracy of self-proclaimed experts indifferent to anything that doesn't match their agenda," he thought angrily. Part of him felt like striking out and another part felt like crying.

After kicking every waste basket in sight, he began formulating his response for the inevitable meeting awaiting him at work. After composing himself, the Journalist drove to the office. He was greeted by a wide-eyed secretary who directed him to the editor immediately upon his arrival.

The Journalist walked in and sat down while the editor completed a phone call. He couldn't help but overhear what was clearly a one-way conversation. The editor kept saying, "Yes, sir, I understand," followed several moments later by, "you make a good point." Finally he said, "Thank you sir, I can assure you we will take your concerns under consideration," and replaced the receiver with exaggerated care.

After a long deep breath he said, "Well, I suppose you could imagine who that was?"

The Journalist nodded.

"His majesty the mayor is pretty upset. He is demanding a retraction, a resignation, and a follow-up article that 'states the facts' in ways that are more consistent with his agenda," said the editor.

"I can't retract the story, sir, but I can understand the pressure you are under and I'm willing to comply with one of his demands," said the Journalist. He reached to the inside pocket of his jacket and held out the hastily written resignation he had prepared earlier that morning.

"Now hold it," said the editor, holding up his hand. "It's not necessary that you do this. Regardless of our beloved mayor's opinion, the media is independent and free to report the facts as we see them. That right is protected under the constitution of our country."

"I know, but that's really not the point, said the Journalist. "The past two years have been extremely hard for me. I've seen too much, reported on issues too troubling, and frankly I'm just spent – burnt out, I guess."

The editor studied the Journalist for several long moments. Silently he recalled similar experiences, similar frustrations and similar decisions in his own life. "You know," he said slowly, "I really do understand."

He paused a moment to look out the window, then turned back to look squarely at the Journalist. "Listen, I don't want whatever you have in your hand. Not right now, anyway."

He leaned across his desk, reaching for a piece of paper. "I read an article recently in a magazine that comes to my home," said the editor. "It told the story of a church right here in our city – one that's a little different than the norm and making a pretty significant impact. Frankly I'm a little skeptical about all of this, but I'll make a deal with you. Research this story, conduct a few interviews, and let me know if it's something worth reporting. After that we can talk some more about what you have in your hand."

" . . .my road to cynicism probably began at church."

The Journalist sighed. "I'm not sure that we're not just post-poning the inevitable," he said, looking down at the piece of paper. "And this church thing doesn't interest me all that much – in fact, my road to cynicism probably began at church."

"What do you mean?" asked the editor.

"To me, it seems that most church goers are just playing the role." He paused, thinking about how to phrase his next statement, "My sister and I used to play house when we were kids. We set up our little make believe house in the upstairs of our garage and we picked a role to play. That pretty much sums up my experience in church."

"Explain a little more what you mean by that," said the editor.

"Well it's all about playing games," the Journalist began, speaking slowly as if trying to decipher vague impressions. "People get dressed in their 'church clothes' and go to church. They act appropriately in that setting, but on Monday it's different."

"What do you mean?"

The Journalist shifted uncomfortably in his chair, becoming sorry he brought up the whole issue. "Oh, it's really nothing I guess," he said. "It just seems to me that if people make a statement about their love for God on Sunday then they ought to live like they love Him on Monday."

A long silence followed his last remark, and the Journalist shifted again in his chair.

"I see," the editor said softly. Then more business-like, "I guess lots of people have those same frustrations, but from all I can gath-

---

"… it seems to me that if people make a statement about their love for God on Sunday then they ought to live like they love Him on Monday."

---

er this church is different. I'm not asking you to write the story, I'm just asking you to do a little research and see if there *is a* story."

The Journalist had been here before. The editor wasn't going to settle for a no answer. "All right," he conceded. "But I'm not throwing away this piece of paper. I'll get back to you within a week."

The editor nodded, a small smile playing at the corners of his mouth. He reached for the copy of the magazine article on his desk and handed it to the Journalist. "Here's something to get you started," he said. "I think you'll find it interesting."

Think About It . . .

1. What words would you use to describe your attitude toward church?

2. What role do you believe God has intended for the church?

3. How would you rate your church's involvement in reaching out to your world?

4. Think about it.

Chapter Two

A Nurse Who Changed

The Journalist read the magazine article. It detailed the story of a growing church in the city, a congregation allegedly filled with people who were clearly different. The article included side bars with stories of individuals in the church who experienced extraordinary change. As a result, community culture was actually changing because of how these same people were interacting with their world.

He jotted notes on a sheet of paper in front of him. Included were the names of some of the people mentioned in the story, the name of the pastor of the church, and notes regarding some of the specific changes that had allegedly occurred in the community.

His attention was particularly drawn to a story of a young nurse who had gotten involved in an area of the city with which he was very familiar. In fact, it was the same area that had been the focus of the feature story that had raised the ire of the mayor. It seemed a good place to start in his research so he picked up the phone on his desk to ask one of the research assistants in the office to search out a number.

The phone was picked up on the first ring. "Hi, this is Lynda," a cheery voice answered.

"Good morning," said the Journalist. He identified himself and his assignment. "I'm wondering if there might be an opportunity for me to sit down with you and learn more about you and some of the work in which you're involved?"

"Of course," she said, without hesitation. "I would love to meet you! In fact I've read just about everything you've written and I am especially intrigued by your last feature. It would be an honor to sit down with you."

"I must admit, that's a bit more enthusiastic a response than I usually get," replied the Journalist. "Usually people think of ways to try to avoid me!"

Lynda laughed. "Well, not me. How about tomorrow afternoon, say 3:00?"

The Journalist arrived at the hospital a few minutes before his scheduled appointment. The freeway traffic had been horrible and he found himself trying to wind down from the stress of negotiating side streets in an effort to be on time. Intrigued by his brief phone conversation, he was growing eager to learn more about the things he had read in the magazine article.

He walked into the hospital cafeteria where they agreed to meet. He unconsciously raked his fingers through his hair when a young nurse approached him. "Hi," she said, "You wouldn't happen to be the Journalist would you?"

"As a matter of fact, I am," he smiled. "I must look like one, huh?"

"Maybe it's the hair," she said, smiling. "I guess everybody has an idea what a journalist must look like – wild hair, sneakers and a legal pad."

"Well, I guess I'm not a disappointment," he answered with a grin.

If the phone conversation had been intriguing, he was totally disarmed by her friendliness. It wasn't forced. Rather she seemed very at ease and comfortable, like someone with whom you could sit down, kick off your shoes, and enjoy a good conversation.

They went through the cafeteria line, picked up some coffee and made their way to a small table in a corner of the room. After taking their seats the Journalist said, "Wow, I'm not sure where to begin. When I read the magazine article I was specifically drawn to the part which explained some of the things you're doing in an area of the city – one I'm especially familiar with."

"I'd say!" she said. "I read your recent feature and was impressed by your insights. I'm surprised you got away with it."

"Well, that's another story for another time," he said. "But back to you right now." The Journalist was not interested in rehearsing the impact of his story with her, at least not now. The magazine sidebar had made specific mention about an extraordinary change that had occurred in Lynda's life and that's where he wanted to begin.

Taking a copy of the article from between the pages of his legal pad he began to speak. "This story is pretty fascinating to me and there are lots of things I would like to know. But one of the most interesting is the reference to a changed life. As I experience you now, I'm wondering what has changed. Were you a wild and loose pagan or something?"

"Well I don't know about wild and loose, but there has been an unbelievable change in my life." Her eyes crinkled slightly in the corners as she smiled. "Change is an interesting word, isn't it? I came into this profession because I wanted to help people but somewhere along the way I lost my passion for it all. God had to intervene in my life or I would have ended it."

"I came into this profession because I wanted to help people but somewhere along the way I lost my passion for it all. God had to intervene in my life or I would have ended it."

"You mean, end your life?" he asked.

"Yes," she said quietly. "I became cold and cynical, not someone to whom you would come for comfort. But God changed all of that."

"I see," he said, caught off guard by her sincerity. "What happened?"

Suddenly aware that his query seemed abrupt, he added in a softer tone, "I mean, what you are saying sounds pretty transforming, especially considering the state in which you described yourself."

"I was invited by a colleague of mine to attend a symposium for medical professionals that was being sponsored and underwritten by Community Church. It had a fascinating title, something like *'Finding Focus When It Makes No Sense'* or something like that. The speaker was a doctor here in the hospital, a man who had already aroused my curiosity."

She paused a moment and then continued, "I don't know, he

is one of those types who has a quiet depth that becomes most apparent when the situations seem most difficult. I was intrigued enough, I guess, to accept the invitation to attend."

"And what happened?" the Journalist prodded.

"I actually don't remember much about all that was said," she said. "Oh, there were notes and everything and obviously a lot of thought went behind the presentation, but what impacted me most was his attitude, his composure, his empathic ways – things like that."

"And . . ." the Journalist urged her to continue.

"There was a time for questions and then the moderator for the evening summed things up. A card was included in the packet of information that had been distributed before the session and we were asked to check boxes on the card if we had any interest in other opportunities the church was providing for the medical community."

". . . it was what wasn't said that impacted me, his attitude, composure, empathic ways . . ."

The Journalist scribbled short notes on a pad. "What kinds of things?" he asked.

"Other symposiums were scheduled quarterly. A newsletter was offered that featured the anecdotal stories of people who have used their professional skills in helping others, things like that."

"What did you do? I mean, did you respond?" the Journalist asked.

"Yes, the topics for the next sessions addressed issues that were of interest to me and I didn't want to miss any of them. The presenters were people well known in our profession, individuals from throughout the country." She smiled that disarming smile again, "It kind of looked like a who's who in the national medical community."

"I'm sure there's more? I mean, if you were once a cynic you sure could have fooled me!"

She nodded. "Oh, there's lots more. In the midst of all of this I found God."

"I didn't know He was missing," said the Journalist then immediately regretted his cynical little quip.

Not offended, Lynda chuckled appreciatively. "He was certainly missing in my life."

Think About It . . .

1. Do you find fulfillment in what you do vocationally?

2. Can you see God at work in your world?

3. What could be different if God were to be a significant part of your workplace experience?

4. Think about it.

Chapter Three

The Pastor

The Journalist found himself unusually disturbed after his meeting with Lynda. She was pleasant enough, in fact, quite charming. Her quiet dignity, sensitivity and gentleness were appealing, as was the warmth of her smile. What disturbed him, however, was the natural ease with which she referred to her "relationship with Christ." What exactly did she mean?

It was an enigma to him – her confident self-assurance, her settled and loving demeanor, the intimate and personal way in which she spoke of Jesus Christ. She tried to explain what she meant, but it was too confusing, too simplistic, and too irrational to satisfy his pragmatic mind.

She mentioned the pastor of Community Church, whom she simply called "Tom," and suggested he might be a better person to talk to about some of his probing questions that her answers didn't seem to satisfy.

He picked up the card she had given him. He reluctantly punched out the numbers on the phone keypad, almost hoping that Tom would be on a long vacation in some remote part of the earth. It would be nice if he could fulfill his commitment to his editor and get on with life without having to delve into something that made him feel this uncomfortable.

"Good afternoon, Community Church, how may I serve you?" the secretary asked, almost too cheerfully.

"Good afternoon," he answered, wishing she hadn't been quite so pleasant, "I'm a journalist with the city newspaper. I've been reading a little about your church and was hoping I might be able to meet with the pastor to ask a few questions."

"Oh yes," the secretary said. "I got a call earlier this week from Lynda over at the hospital telling me you might contact us. Tom is out right now, but he told me before he left that if you were interested in visiting, he would be pleased to meet with you on Thursday morning."

"Thursday morning works for me," said the Journalist. "How about 10:00?"

"You've got it," she replied. "I've got it marked in his calendar. Do you need directions?"

"No, I've driven by the church. I shouldn't have any problem at all."

On Thursday the Journalist felt a strange sense of excitement and dread – like he was going to the dentist with a toothache, looking forward to being relieved of the pain but not terribly excited about the process. Feeling strangely stirred, he acknowledged to himself that the smiling nurse had uncovered a sensitive nerve. She had a simple, yet powerful faith in the work of a Person who lived 2,000 years ago. He heard it, understood the words, but was unable to make sense of it.

On his drive to the church building he absently raked his fingers through his hair several times. He frowned, realizing he was struggling to separate himself and his needs from his instinct to objectively observe and report.

He walked into a spacious front office just as a middle aged man walked through the door. He smiled broadly as he extended his hand, "Hi, I'm Tom. What can I do to help you?"

The Journalist introduced himself sharing that he was doing research on a possible story about Community Church. "I'm here to meet the pastor to fill in some empty spaces in my research."

Tom smiled. "Well that would be me," he said. "Let's walk back to my office."

The Journalist was embarrassed. Somehow he didn't make the connection between this Tom and the one he had come to visit. He wasn't expecting someone in a casual shirt and slacks, he wasn't sure why. "Oh, I'm sorry," he said, "I guess I was expecting someone in black and a clerical collar." The words sounded awkward in his own ears.

"Oh, that's fine. We're pretty casual around here," Tom said, dismissing the remark.

They walked into the pastor's office. Two walls were lined

with books, one was a bank of windows overlooking an atrium filled with flowers, and the other wall was one big white board with lots of ideas scribbled all over.

"Have a seat," Tom said directing the Journalist to a sofa in the middle of the room. Tom walked to his desk, glanced over some papers before sitting down in the overstuffed chair opposite the sofa. He stretched out his legs in front of him and asked, "Now what can I do to help you?"

The Journalist explained the assignment he had received from his editor and reported what he knew, in broad terms, about the church and its work. He mentioned the fact that he had visited with Lynda without revealing too much about their conversation.

"Lynda – what a great gal," said Tom reflectively. "Let me tell you, her story is something else. If you had met her a year ago you would find it hard to believe she is the same person."

"That's what . . . church is all about. It's not about numbers, it's not about programs, it's about restoring a relationship between God and people that was broken as a result of sin."

"She shared some of her story with me," said the Journalist. "She kept talking about all the changes that had occurred in her life, ascribing them to a work that God did in her heart."

"Absolutely," said Tom. "And that's what Community Church is all about. It's not about numbers, it's not about programs – it's about restoring a relationship between God and people that was broken as a result of sin. Lynda is only one example of hundreds that I could introduce you to whose lives have been transformed through the relationship made possible between God and man through what His Son, Jesus Christ accomplished on the cross."

"Sounds kind of complicated to me," said the Journalist. "I've seen some pretty hard cases in the course of my career and I've pretty much given up on God."

"And so had Lynda," Tom replied nonplussed. "There have been hundreds of others like her in our church – who had given up and had become cynical and hardened. What has happened in their lives is only attributable to God."

"You mean, you don't take credit for it?"

Tom smiled. "No, not at all. This is a special place, though, where people care about one another and God is actively at work in a variety of ways. People are engaged with one another, reaching out individually and collectively into their worlds. Change is taking place – not because of us, but because people have made themselves available to God and utilize their special abilities to serve God throughout this community."

Although struck by the passion that accompanied the words, the Journalist remained skeptical. "This all sounds good, but don't you imagine that there are any number of churches and organizations in our city that might claim the same thing?" he asked.

"Perhaps," said Tom. "I really don't know. I do know that God has given our church a mandate to reach our world with the redemptive message of His love. We're not leaving that job to someone else; we're assuming it as the work He called us to do."

The Journalist snorted. "A rather bold resolve, don't you think?"

"I supposed it could be construed that way," said Tom. "However, it seems to me that there is a prevailing attitude in the world that the needs of people are the responsibility of someone else. We don't make that assumption."

Tom sat up straight in his chair and leaned forward. "We've taken a different tack, one we believe is consistent with the commands of God's Word. We operate from a position of pro-activity, reaching out in a variety of ways to our various communities, presenting God's love and work to others through our actions as well as our words." Tom's conviction and earnestness communicated as eloquently as the words themselves.

The Journalist stared hard at him for a moment. Finally he said, "I'm not sure that's what I expected to hear. I must admit that I'm curious to learn more about the process and how you are executing these initiatives, given the size and diversity of the people who worship here."

"The Church is bigger than this physical place," said Tom, motioning with his hand to the area immediately around him. "It is made up of people worldwide who have been rescued and who have responded in faith to the provisions of God through His Son Jesus Christ. It is the Church which reflects the image of God in our world, and it is our belief that it is the people who make up the Church who must take the lead in addressing the issues that have been created as a result of sin."

"Whoa," the Journalist said. He stopped scribbling for a moment and held up his right hand, pen still between his fingers. "I'm trying to get all this down and comprehend it at the same time. This isn't exactly stuff that I hear from people everyday. Most of my acquaintances either ignore the troubling issues that exist within their world or pass them off as the responsibilities of someone else."

"It is our belief that it is the people who make up the Church who must take the lead in addressing the issues that have been created as a result of sin."

"That's just it," Tom declared. "That's exactly the issue. And while we're not using our position in the community to browbeat others into seeing things 'our way,' we are committed to fulfilling our responsibilities as Christians in this world."

"I understand, or at least I think I do," said Journalist haltingly, as if trying to convince himself that he did.

"Listen, I've got the time if you have the interest," said Tom. "I would be happy to meet with you over the next few weeks and walk you through how we do this. You might find it interesting."

"That would be great, but why would you take so much time with me?" asked the Journalist, not seeing the profit in it for Tom.

Tom looked him directly in the eye. "This is a message that's worth being told," he said. "It isn't about us – it isn't about our congregation. It's much bigger than that. I'm convinced that if the Church would make note of what is beginning to happen here, then God could use us to facilitate change that goes beyond addressing surface needs to impacting the very hearts of men and women. It might actually spark a spiritual reawakening in the world!"

"I'm convinced that if the Church would make note of what is beginning to happen here, God could use us to facilitate change that goes beyond addressing surface needs to impacting the very hearts of men and women. It might actually spark a spiritual reawakening in the world!"

"That sounds rather ambitious to me," chuckled the Journalist, still not entirely sure he grasped the concept. "I think we need to meet and talk again before we make any long term commitment of our time."

"Fair enough," said Tom. "Let's meet again next week and see what happens."

Think About It . . .

1. If you were to describe the relationship you have with your church, what words would come to mind?

2. Based on your experience, write a mission statement that reflects the mission of your church?

3. Is your mission statement consistent with how Tom describes the mission of Community Church?

4. Think about it.

Chapter Four

A Relationship Restored

Two days later the Journalist called Tom to schedule their next meeting, pleasantly surprised when Tom greeted him enthusiastically and was willing to adjust his calendar to accommodate their time together. They planned to meet a week from Thursday.

As the day of the meeting drew closer, the Journalist found himself becoming apprehensive. He liked Tom and he felt comfortable with him. He was easy to talk to and seemed eager to share his passion with others. But in Tom's presence he felt uncomfortable – a kind of emptiness that he couldn't quite pinpoint. It was as if he had a thirst for something that couldn't be quenched.

On his way to the meeting, he drove unusually slow, pondering the upcoming discussion as he turned the corner into the church parking lot. He took a deep breath as he exited the car and made his way across the parking lot.

Tom was standing by his desk when the Journalist was escorted into his office by the church secretary. Grinning broadly, Tom walked from the desk and extending his hand.

"Great to see you again," he exclaimed, gripping his hand firmly. "I've been really looking forward to our meeting today." His words seemed genuine.

"It's good to see you again Tom" said the Journalist. I've been thinking a lot about today and, well, I guess I'm glad to be here too."

"You guess?" Tom smiled. "Come on, sit down, we've got a lot to talk about."

The Journalist walked over to the sofa just as the secretary walked in with two cups of steaming coffee. "I thought we could enjoy some refreshment as we think through some things together," said Tom. The Journalist reached for a cup of coffee, adding a small envelope of sugar into the dark, steaming liquid.

Tom began without pretense. "You implied you had some reticence in coming today. What's that all about?"

"That's not so easy to answer," said the Journalist, wondering how to express what he felt without sounding absurd. "I enjoyed our last visit, but in preparing for this time I experienced a funny feeling that I am finding difficult to explain. It's like I'm thirsty and nothing that I can do seems to satisfy that thirst. I know that sounds weird, but it's the best I can do."

"That doesn't sound weird at all," said Tom. "I remember a time I felt the same way and it wasn't until I understood what was going on that I found the relief I longed for."

"What do you mean?"

"God wants more than anything to have a personal, intimate relationship with you. And He wanted it so much that He was willing to let His only Son pay the penalty for your sins on the cross."

"Well, let me begin somewhere else," said Tom. He reached to a table next to his chair and picked up a well worn Bible. "This book tells a remarkable story, and the entire message can be summed up in the context of relationship. It begins by telling the story of a relationship between God and man that was severed as a result of sin and the remaining pages talk about God reaching out to men throughout history. The story leads to Jesus, God's only Son, who made it possible for the severed relationship to be permanently restored."

"Okay, but what's that got to do with my feelings?"

"Everything!" said Tom. "You see, there is nothing in man that naturally desires to restore that broken relationship between himself and God. Only God's Spirit can convict someone of sin and produce a desire to know Him."

He paused for a moment to glance at the Journalist before adding, "My guess is that God is beginning to create that hunger in your heart."

Brows furrowed as the Journalist pondered Tom's explanation.

He didn't understand all the references to God, His Son, and all the jargon, like 'conviction,' but that didn't matter because something seemed to resonate inside him.

"That's interesting," he finally blurted out, not really knowing what else to say. "If what you say is true, though, what am I supposed to do about it?"

"It's important that you know what God did to restore a relationship with you," said Tom.

"With me? Are you trying to tell me that God desires a relationship with me?" The Journalist shook his head.

"That's exactly what I am saying," said Tom. "In fact, God wants more than anything to have a personal, intimate relationship with you. And He wants that so much that He was willing to let His only Son pay the death penalty for your sins on the cross."

"I know something about the cross, at least I've seen pictures of it. But what exactly really happened there?" the Journalist asked.

" . . . the quenching of the thirst of your soul can only be satisfied in Christ."

"The perfect Son of God freely and willingly took your sin – and my sin, and the sins of all men – upon Himself, and paid the death penalty required by God on your behalf." Tom paused long enough to let the significance of the incredible gospel message penetrate the heart of this searcher.

"The quenching of the thirst of your soul can only be satisfied in Christ," he continued. "All you have to do is recognize that you are lost without Christ and receive His incredible gift."

The whole concept of God providing forgiveness of sin was staggering to the Journalist. He found himself distraught with grief over the awfulness of what was inside of him. He hadn't thought of it in terms of 'sin' but there was a residual frustration he regularly felt when in the quieter moments of his life he was left to contemplate who he really was.

He put on a good show to the outside world but there was a nagging unsettledness that plagued him, exasperation over his inability to cope with passions he couldn't control, and irritation over the little games he played to gain advantage over others. And now the terrible weight of it all came over him like a dark blanket. He couldn't imagine God ever wanting anything to do with him and now Tom was telling him about a gift that was his if he would open his heart and receive it.

"Receive? Like a gift?" The Journalist shook his head again. "I can't believe God wouldn't require more than that of me."

Tom flipped purposefully the pages of his Bible. He leaned over with the book opened and said, "It is exactly that, the greatest gift ever given. Listen to this: 'For by grace are you saved, through faith, and that not of yourself it is the gift of God, not of works lest any man should boast.'"[1]

"Wow," the Journalist said quietly, almost lost in his own introspection. The very thought of freedom from the horrible guilt of his sin was more than he could comprehend. "You mean there's not a thing I can do but receive the gift?"

"That's pretty much the way it is," Tom replied, leaning back in his chair. "Salvation from our sin is totally the work of God. You can't earn it, money can't buy it and position means nothing in obtaining it. It's *totally* the work of God. He gives us what we don't deserve and He graciously withholds from us all that we do deserve – that's 'grace' and 'mercy,' and this message is called the 'Good News'."

"Good news," the Journalist whispered, "I guess it is pretty good news." He felt both terrible grief over his sinful condition and a rising excitement in the hope that the nagging pain this sin had caused could somehow be permanently relieved. "How do I receive a gift that I can't touch or see?"

"By telling God you would like to receive the gift. It's as simple as that. Would you like to do that?" Tom asked.

"Yes, I would." The Journalist could hardly believe how quickly the words flew out of his mouth. The nagging in his heart seemed strangely satisfied and he felt a new feeling, a peace he had ever known in his life. "How do I do it?"

Tom smiled and reached for his hand, "Why don't we tell God that we recognize our sin and realize we can do absolutely nothing to earn His favor and tell Him that we receive His gift of sal-

1. Ephesians 2:8-9

vation accomplished through Christ on the cross?"

They bowed their heads and Tom prayed aloud, "Lord Jesus, I thank you that I can come to You and talk to You this way. I'm so grateful for what You've done for me in giving me life in You. I ask You now for my new friend that he, too, might find peace and life in You."

Tom stopped and said to the Journalist, "Why don't you tell God what's on your heart right now."

The Journalist closed his eyes and tears flowed down his face.

"God," he stammered, "I have done nothing to deserve this opportunity. I have sinned terribly in my life and there's nothing within me that deserves a relationship with You. Please forgive me."

Here he stopped for a few moments and wept silently. When he regained control he added, "I do receive this gift of life You have made possible to me through the sacrifice You made for me by dying for my sin."

There was a long pause, then Tom quietly said, "Amen."

Think About It . . .

1. What words would you use to describe your personal relationship with Jesus Christ?

2. Who can you best relate to in the story: The Journalist, Lynda, or Tom?

3. Do you believe that there are answers for life's most troubling issues in Christ?

4. Think about it.

Chapter Five

Community Church

The next week was one of the most extraordinary weeks of the Journalist's life. He felt "clean" for the first time that he could remember – a cleanness which came from the forgiveness of sin he received when Christ entered his life.

Things changed. Dramatically. Generally perceived by those who knew him as melancholic, a personality transformation began to reveal itself in genuine smiles, a new concern for others and an ever-eager recounting to anyone who might listen of how he had found a new life in Christ.

"the peace. . . was the particular transformation he wanted to share with others."

There was also the peace. For the past several years a storm brewed in his soul; a dark, swirling maelstrom that dissipated the moment he lifted his head in Tom's office after that momentous 'Amen.' It was the peace he found most difficult to explain to his friends, but it was this incredible serenity of heart that was the particular transformation he wanted to share with others.

The Journalist met with his editor the day after his visit with Tom. He rehearsed some of his research but confessed that he might find it difficult to report objectively of the things happening at Community Church. The editor merely smiled, and encouraged him to continue his research on the church and its work in the community.

His next appointment with Tom was set for early the following week. The Journalist could hardly wait to report all the things which had occurred in his life since their last time together.

On the day of their scheduled meeting he arrived early. Remembering his apprehension of less than a week before, the Journalist smiled as he made his way to the office.

"Good afternoon," he said, greeting the church secretary cheerily. "Hope things are going well for you today."

The secretary returned his smile. "Yes, it is a nice day isn't it? I think Tom is expecting you, why don't you go right in. I'll bring some coffee in just a few moments."

"That'd be great," The journalist replied. "And thanks so much for your thoughtfulness." As he spoke the words he smiled again, thinking it was the first time he could remember making a statement like that.

Tom opened the door before the Journalist got to turn the knob. "I thought that was you I heard," he said. "I must say I had to listen twice before I recognized the lightness of your voice."

"Tom, something seriously significant has happened to me. I mean, serious!" said the Journalist emphatically. "I walked in here last week ready to give up on life, but I walked out with a peace that I can't even explain to the people who are constantly asking what in the world has happened to me! My whole outlook on life has changed – the trees look greener, I even see people differently. I find myself wanting to talk to people rather than trying to escape them."

Tom listened, smiling at the rate in which the words seem to tumble out as the new Christian told his story. "The Bible calls it new birth," he answered gently. "When you received Christ's gift to you last week you became like a new born baby."

Tom reached for a Bible and quickly found the verse he was looking for, "The Bible describes it this way, 'When someone becomes a Christian he becomes a brand new person inside. He is not the same any more. A new life has begun!'"[1]

"Wow, that's exactly what happened," said the Journalist. "I feel like I've got a new lease on life, like everything is beginning all over again."

"It has, and that's what is behind all that you initially heard about Community Church and its work in this city," said Tom. "Our church is composed of people just like you – people who

1. 2 Corinthians 5:17

have found real life in Christ and realize that they have something to share that can transform the lives of others as well. And as others are changed, they honestly believe that they can be used of God in making a difference in facilitating meaningful change in their world."

"You're talking about people like Lynda, right?"

"Absolutely. Lynda is just one of hundreds who have experienced what it means to be in relationship with Christ. Her life has changed and taken on new meaning. She's now being used of the Lord to make a difference in the lives of others through her work as a nurse."

"I know," said the Journalist. "She tried to explain that all to me but it just didn't make sense at the time. I'm beginning to put it all together now and I'm starting to feel an excitement about my new life and what it might end up looking like."

Tom felt elation in his own heart at the words of his new friend. It was a scene he had enjoyed before and one that he never tired of experiencing. "The Bible says that those who are part of God's family are members of His church.[1] And God has chosen to use the church to accomplish His work in our world," he said.

"You mean Community Church?"

Tom paused a moment. "Yes and no," he said. "Every person who has ever received Christ's gift of salvation from the penalty of their sin is a member of the Church, regardless of where they live. That's like Church with a capital 'C'. Our church body here represents an assembly of those who have invited Christ into their life here within our community."

"You mean Community Church is a small 'c' church, right?"

"Exactly. We're just one of thousands of churches located in places all around the world. Some meet in buildings like ours, others meet in homes, some in dark jungles in remote corners of the earth, and still others meet in hiding, fearing reprisal from those who would destroy them and the work they are trying to do."

"You mean that still happens in our enlightened world?" The Journalist asked the question only half in jest.

Tom grew serious. "Unfortunately, yes. There are still many

1. I Corinthians 12:28

43

places in the world where Christians are persecuted yet they still gather, often in hiding, and still diligently persist in sharing their faith in Christ with others regardless of the price they might have to pay."

"That's amazing but I can understand better now that it would be pretty hard to be quiet about a change as significant as what has taken place in my life."

"You're right," Tom nodded. "The message of salvation through Christ's work on the cross is called 'the gospel' in the Bible. That means 'good news.'"

"It's good news all right! In fact it is the best news I have ever heard."

"We're just one of thousands of churches . . . some meet in buildings like ours, others meet in homes, some in dark jungles in remote corners of the earth, and still others meet in hiding, fearing reprisal from those who would destroy them and the work they are trying to do."

The Journalist couldn't totally understand all that had happened to him but he was beginning to comprehend that the same thing has happened to millions of others over the centuries. Images of pictures he had seen in history books of martyrs who willingly died for their faith now began to make some sense. A price had been paid by many to propagate this gospel of which Tom spoke.

There was so much he wanted to learn. "I want to know so much more about Community Church and its work," said the Journalist earnestly. "I mean, I met Lynda and I experienced a tiny bit of what she is doing. She spoke of a doctor that had really impacted her life. What is behind all of this?"

"A plan," Tom immediately answered. "We know what the church should be doing and we are committed to doing it. The Scripture is quite clear on what our role should be. As we see it the Church has both an external mandate, that is to share this gospel message to people here in our community and around the world and an internal mandate to train and equip those within the church to fulfill God's will that others know what has been accomplished on their behalf through Christ's work on the cross." Tom opened his Bible and read from Matthew 28: 19-20, Acts 1:8, and Ephesians 4.

"You know," Tom smiled, "I have lots of images in my mind of the church. One of them is like an emergency clinic; a place where people come to get bandaged up from the battle scars of the week, to be encouraged, supported, and loved by others. And then I think of the church as a rehabilitation clinic, a place where people can come and be equipped to serve God more effectively where they live in fulfilling the responsibilities that God has given to us."

Tom spoke as one driven. Beyond his calm demeanor, there was a fire ablaze in his soul that caused him to commit his time and resources to a task so much bigger than himself.

"Our church leadership team has drawn a circle around the boundaries of our city and we have said that we are claiming this city for our Lord."

Tom continued, "Recognizing these mandates, our church leadership team has taken a highlight pen and has drawn a circle around the boundaries of our city and we have said that we are claiming this city for our Lord. We are working to mobilize our church members in a variety of ways in accomplishing this goal. We don't intend to willingly relinquish this incredible opportunity God has graciously granted us to make a difference in our world."

"That's what I want to learn more about – and frankly, I don't want to be left out," said the Journalist "For the last several years I found myself becoming increasingly cynical about the world. I reported things that I thought would cause people to think, deplorable situations in our own community that need to be addressed. The net result was pretty much zero. No one seemed to care; no one wanted to get their hands dirty helping someone else."

Tom nodded in agreement. "You're right, we need to get our hands dirty. But all the work in the world outside the context of relationship is going to have minimal impact. That's why we have created a model for ministry that focuses on building relational networks which grant us a platform on which we can share our faith and the difference Christ can make."

The Journalist felt hope beginning to bud in his heart. There might actually be some answers after all. Tom spoke with such conviction about the work of people who ministered at Community Church. Suddenly the Journalist found himself wanting to be part of this church body, working alongside others to communicate the 'good news' and address those issues which so dramatically impact the actual culture of a community.

"The initial purpose of my meeting with you was to learn about Community Church and what made it different," said the

---

". . . society has become complacent, looking to everyone else – particularly the government – to resolve all the problems."

Journalist. "My job was to do an in-depth story of a church making a difference. You need to know that because I want to ask you about your plan, the relational model you just told me about and how it works. Maybe my paper will print the story, maybe it won't. But I am determined to write it because it will help me to understand how I can become involved."

Tom seemed nonplussed by the confession. "Your honesty becomes you," he said. "We are not trying to keep our ministry a secret. In fact, we want as many people as possible to know what we're doing. Our society has become complacent, looking to everyone else – particularly the government – to resolve all the problems. I believe differently. I believe the Lord called the Church to be His witness in the world. He called believers to minister to others and to be a witness to them. That's not accomplished at home in front of the television. It requires people to recognize their responsibility, exercise their giftedness and 'get their hands dirty.' And we're committed to leading the way by example."

"When do we begin?" asked the Journalist.

"How about next week?"

Think About It . . .

1. Can you relate to the peace that The Journalist found in a relationship with Christ?

2. Write a description of what you believe your community would look like in 20 years if the church of which you are a part were to be 100% successful in fulfilling its mission.

3. Are you prepared to "get your hands dirty" in facilitating some of the changes you recognized?

4. Think about it.

Chapter Six

Relationships

They scheduled their next meeting at a local coffee shop on the edge of the city. It was a relaxing haunt for the college crowd, a place with deep stuffed chairs, dimmed lights and high speed internet connections. They arrived within minutes of each other and ordered their respective lattés.

Steaming cups in hand, the two maneuvered through the chairs and gangly outstretched legs to two large overstuffed leather chairs in a distant corner of the room.

"I've been thinking about how to share all of this with you in a way that makes the most sense," Tom began. "There are a lot of things we do at Community Church and they all have purpose behind them. But what's behind it all is the superseding conviction that effective ministry is rooted in the context of relationships."

"…effective ministry is rooted in the context of relationships."

"You inferred that during our initial visit," said the Journalist, taking a sip of his coffee. "Share more with me about what you mean."

"Well, think about someone with whom you have a treasured relationship. As you reflect on that relationship, what are some of the words that come to mind when trying to describe it?"

The Journalist thought for a moment. "Well, I'd think of words like trust, fun, caring, acceptance, honest, integrity. Things like that."

"Exactly. You trust your friends, you enjoy being with them, they genuinely care about you and you care about them. These are special qualities and we don't experience them with everybody like we do with our friends."

The Journalist raised his eyebrows. "That's true. In fact, there are not many people I can think of with whom I even have that kind of relationship. It takes a lot of time to cultivate."

"That's a good point," said Tom. "You must choose to move into relationship with someone else, and that choice requires an investment of your time. The wonderful virtues you named don't just occur overnight."

"You're right about that. But it's worth it."

"It is worth it," said Tom. "And think about this – who benefits from a good relationship?"

The Journalist's eyebrows shot up again. "Is this a trick question? Of course both of us benefit."

". . . outside of relationship, a lot of what God commands us to do has minimal impact. Too often we're so intent on an agenda that we miss the people along the way. They feel bypassed, missed, unnecessary, maybe even used to make someone else feel good."

"No, I wasn't intending to trick you, but it's interesting that most people don't think of that. Too often people want something from someone else and they work hard to get it. If their agenda is not forthcoming, they walk away and look to another. Few people want to take the time to build the kinds of relationships that mirror the words you mentioned in describing the ideal. In true relationships both parties benefit, otherwise it wouldn't be a relationship," Tom smiled that disarming smile.

"I suppose that's true, but what does that have to do with impacting the lives of people?" asked the Journalist.

"Actually, everything," said Tom. "As I said earlier, ministry is most effectively accomplished in the context of relationship." He reached inside his jacket pocket and pulled out a diminutive New Testament and thumbed through the pages. "In some of the letters that the Apostle Paul wrote he give instructions to

Christians, such as, 'Be devoted to one another,'[1] and, 'Bear one another's burdens.'[2] There are lots of these kinds of commands."

Tom placed the small volume back into his pocket. "Now those are nice things to do, but if I were to come up to you as a perfect stranger, pat you on the back and tell you I'm devoted to you – just what kind of impact would that have?"

"Not much," the Journalist admitted. "I guess I would appreciate the thought but I certainly wouldn't walk away feeling like my burden was lifted."

"I'm sure you wouldn't. Do you see why outside of relationship, a lot of what God commands us to do has minimal impact? Too often we're so intent on our agenda that we miss people along the way. They feel bypassed, missed, unnecessary, maybe even used to make someone else feel good."

The Journalist could think of several times when he had those exact feelings – times when he felt someone pursued a relationship only to find out that he or she wanted something that he was unable to give. When the person figured that out, that was the end of that.

"The truths of God's Word are not abstract – they can only be experienced as live and impacting within in the context of relationship."

"I can definitely relate to that."

"We all can," said Tom. "But that's perhaps a characteristic of our society. It's no wonder that the Church struggles to make the kind of impact it desires. We are reluctant to move into relationships. And the sad fact is, how we relate to others is often an indicator of how we relate to God."

"It's still hard for me to think about relating to God," said the Journalist. "I mean, God – the whole idea of relating to God – is beyond my comprehension."

"I understand, but God wants to have a relationship with you," said Tom. "He's designed you for a relationship with

1. I Corinthians 16:15
2. Galatians 6:2

Him. That's what was lost in the Garden of Eden when Eve and Adam sinned and what was made possible for us through Christ's death on the cross."

"That's awesome!" the Journalist exclaimed. "You mean I can talk to God? That He will communicate with me? That I can enjoy a personal, ongoing relationship with the creator of the universe?"

"Absolutely!" Tom smacked his free hand on his knee. "Within that relationship you will develop, you will grow in your love for God. You will begin to comprehend God's incredible love for you. He desired a relationship with you so much that He sent His Son to die for you. In the context of relationship, everything makes much more sense."

"So you're telling me that a primary focus of Community Church is to bring people into relationship with Christ and one another?" This was a lot of new information and the Journalist wanted to make sure he understood.

"In the context of relationship, everything makes sense."

"Yes, because we can't expect to really impact our world from a distance," said Tom. "It involves making choices to get to know people, committing ourselves to them and sacrificing things in the interest of others. These are not easy things, but when we make the effort, we begin to see changes in our lives and in the lives of others. The truths of God's Word are not abstract – they can only be experienced as alive and impacting within the context of relationship."

The Journalist frowned as a new thought occurred to him. "How can you accomplish all that strategically? I mean, aren't relationships a spontaneous thing?"

Tom nodded. "Of course, but you make choices. Sometimes those choices are based on your needs, sometimes they are based on other factors. I can choose to build relationships with individuals in the inner city, I can choose to build relationships with individuals in this room."

"Yes, you could. But they must choose, too, if there's going to be a relationship. Right?"

"Exactly, and not everyone will choose that," said Tom. "However, they will rarely ever choose if they aren't approached and given a choice."

"A good point," said the Journalist, tapping his pencil on the tablet in front of him. "So the key to the Community Church approach is relationships. What's next?"

Tom smiled. "The next thing we need to talk about is giftedness. You see every Christian has been uniquely gifted by God. And God intends for you to use your gift to serve Him and to minister to others." He looked at his watch then back at the Journalist. "I think that discussion will have to be over another cup of coffee."

Think About It . . .

1. List the names of individuals with whom you have a warm, intimate, fulfilling relationship.

2. What words would you use to describe why these relationships are so fulfilling?

3. Are you willing to make choices and sacrifices to pursue relationships for the cause of Christ?

4. Think about it.

❖ Chapter Seven

Incomplete by Design

During every free moment The Journalist found himself devouring God's Word. He took a highlight pen and each time he discovered a new truth, he made a point to highlight it in a brilliant fluorescent color. Soon the pages of his Bible, complete with coffee stains, looked more fluorescent than black and white.

Many times he would just close his eyes, exhausted, contemplating God and all that He had done to pursue and rescue people. He questioned what could possibly cause anyone to refuse what God offered through Christ. He recognized the power of sin and its stranglehold. He wanted to grab people and shake them to get their attention so he could tell them they didn't need to live lives of quiet desperation, that the answers to their yearnings could be found in a person – in a relationship with Jesus Christ.

"When you understand the control that sin has on a person's life, it makes you even more aware of God's overwhelming power and His immense love. Salvation in Christ is totally the work of God!"

He and Tom had agreed to meet at the coffee shop again, and as the Journalist pulled into a parking space he could see Tom walking across the parking lot. He called out and Tom waited for him and together they made their way for their meeting.

"Hey, Tom, take a look at this," the Journalist grappled with the case he had in his hand as Tom opened the door and made his way to the long line to place their order. The Journalist pulled his Bible out of the case. He opened it and flipped through the pages.

"Do you know, in the last month I have read through the New Testament three times?" he asked. "Look at these marks."

He pointed to the fluorescent highlights throughout the text. "I've marked every passage that I have found that speaks specifically of God's love and pursuit of people. As I read them, and re-read them, I can hardly believe how anyone could repeatedly close their eyes to the obvious. Why?"

As the Journalist spoke his voice became increasingly louder and many of those in line looked over at them curiously.

"The Bible talks about the depravity of man," said Tom. "Man is born in sin and he lives his life committed to it. Only God can break the hold that sin has on the heart of people." As he spoke, they made their way to the head of the line and ordered their drinks. Tom continued to talk as they walked through the maze of people, chairs, and legs. "It's interesting, isn't it? When you understand the control that sin has on a person's life, it makes you even more aware of God's overwhelming power and His immense love. Salvation in Christ is *totally* the work of God."

"No one is ordinary in the sight of God""

"I'm beginning to understand that," said the Journalist. "I can't tell you the times I've asked myself, 'Why me?' And then I feel like I can't do too much for God given all that He has done for me."

"A proper response, I think, for the redeemed!" said Tom.

They found two chairs and settled down and Tom continued. "God has equipped you to serve him. He's equipped me in unique ways, too. You see, we're all kind of wired differently and that is by God's design."

"Are you saying that God intentionally made us that way?"

"Yes – and that's kind of interesting isn't it?" Tom replied with a wry smile. "God designed us to need one another and never is that more evident than in His Church."

He paused. Years of ministry had cemented his conviction that the mandates of the church, to evangelize and to disciple, could only be accomplished as individuals within the church exercised their collective gifts and ministered to others in ways compatible with the resources granted to them by God. He reached for his New Testament and opened it.

"There are two intriguing passages in the New Testament, both of which speak to the matter of spiritual giftedness," he said, turning to the book of Romans and reading from the twelfth chapter. "'God has given each of us the ability to do certain things well.' Isn't that interesting? We all have a special gift from God. There are some things God has given you a unique ability to do and you do it better than almost anyone."

"That is so interesting," said the Journalist thoughtfully. "I'm not sure what that gift might be, though. I'm pretty ordinary."

"No one is ordinary in the sight of God," said Tom. "I'm sure that over time many people have come to you and complimented you on something you do. Have you ever listened to those compliments and wondered what in the world they are talking about?"

"Yes, I guess so," said the Journalist. "Someone recently told me that I have a unique ability to see beyond the obvious. I remember responding with something like, 'You've got to be kidding! It's like seeing something written on a billboard! How could you possibly miss it?'"

"I'm not surprised," said Tom. "The things that we are most often recognized for are the things that come the easiest to us. And I have come to believe that this is the key to understanding what your spiritual gift is."

Turning to another section of the Bible, Tom pointed to a verse in 1 Corinthians 12. "This passage lists several gifts that God gave to the church," he said. The gifts are likened to parts of the body. It's an interesting list, but obviously not a complete one. In fact, the writer says that some gifts are perceived as desirable while others are not. Those he calls 'unseemly,' but points out that both are necessary if the body is to function efficiently."

"Actually, I remember reading that. I just figured that those 'unseemly' parts of the body are like the pancreas or some bile ducts – things like that," said the Journalist with a laugh.

"That may be true but I sure wouldn't want to live without them, would you?"

"I'm not sure what they do, but I imagine if they didn't work, I might understand more!"

"And that's the point," said Tom. "Every part of the body is essential. When parts of the body don't work as they are designed, the whole body suffers.

"You know," he added, "I have come to believe that the dysfunctionality of so many churches today may be based on the fact that there are people within them that fail to exercise or are denied the opportunity to exercise their spiritual giftedness to further God's kingdom."

"Do you mean they refuse to?" the Journalist asked.

". . . the dysfunctionality of so many churches today may be based on the fact that there are people within them that fail to exercise or are denied the opportunity to exercise their spiritual giftedness to further God's kingdom."

"Well in some cases, that is undoubtedly true, but they may be never given the opportunity," said Tom. "Think of this – if you are operating outside your giftedness you might be preventing someone to do what they can do far better than you."

The Journalist was intrigued. He was developing an image in his mind of frustrated people seeing needs and being incapable of dealing with them, and another group of people stressed to the hilt doing things they were never intended or designed to do.

"So what is the answer?," he asked, recognizing the problem.

"I believe the answer is obvious: identify your gift and exercise it," said Tom. "Sounds too simple, doesn't it? But Scripture supports the idea that whenever God calls a work together, He provides all the giftedness that will be required for that work to be successful."

Tom spoke with conviction, but his tone also reflected a certain sense of frustration. He could see a church filled with people who had an incredible task in front of them, yet provided with all the resources to address it – and failing to do so.

A period of silence followed as men were caught up in their thoughts. Then Tom continued. "We have made an effort to help people understand their gifts and then work with them to investigate opportunities where they might be able to use them in ministering to others."

"How can I find my gift?" asked the Journalist.

"Well, begin with listening," said Tom. "Listen to other people – what do they say you do well? Think of what they say, and when it seems almost ridiculous because what they say is so easy to you, ask yourself, 'Could this be God's gift to me?'"

"And then what?"

"Then ask yourself the bigger question, 'How can I use my gift to serve Christ?'"

Think About It . . .

1. List some of the things you have often heard from people acknowledging things you do exceptionally well.

2. Alongside each thing you listed above, write down a number from 1-10 that describes the ease in which you do these things. 1 would represent absolutely no effort and 10 would represent a great deal of effort.

3. Make a list of those things that you gave a score of 5 or less in the space below. Next to them answer the question, how could I use this "gift" to further the cause of the Kingdom of God.

4. Share your ideas with someone else.

5. Think about it.

Chapter Eight

The Vision

The Journalist attended Community Church for two consec-
utive weeks. On his first visit he was warmly welcomed and
introduced to several people, all of whom seemed genuinely
pleased to see him. In fact, a group of singles about his age invited him to lunch after the service.

There was something about the church that he recognized as
different from others he'd attended in the past. He had given up
on the church when he was in high school, having determined
that it was irrelevant to him. Despite that long-standing conclusion, he would visit congregations periodically to ascertain
whether anything had changed. Nothing altered his original
conclusion – until now. Community Church was filled with people who cared for one another, were interested in all that was
taking place and even seemed to enjoy being at the service.

---

*"He had given up on the church when he was in high
school, having determined that the church
was irrelevant to him."*

He remembered a visit to a church several months before. He
went at the invitation of a girl he was dating and didn't win any
points with her when he told her that he met only two people
out of two hundred who didn't have scowls on their faces. He
saw many of them huddled in their little groups looking suspi-
ciously at anyone they didn't immediately recognize. As he
shared his experiences he was reminded that most of the people
he was referring to had been in that church all of their lives and
were perceived by the others as the church cornerstones.

It was their last date.

The Journalist was anxious to visit with Tom again. He was eager to hear his explanation as to what was behind the differences at Community Church.

Their next meeting was scheduled at Tom's home. Nestled among ancient oak trees at the end of a cul-de-sac in a modest development, the white Cape Cod seemed welcoming with its white picket fence and brick driveway. He strolled up to the front door and used the brass knocker to signal his arrival.

Tom's wife, an attractive, smiling woman dressed in jeans and a loose sweater, opened the door. The Journalist introduced himself.

"Oh, it's so good to actually meet you," she said, greeting him with a warm handshake. "Tom has told me a lot about you and the incredible changes occurring in your life. How thrilling!"

She glanced down at her attire. "Forgive my appearance. I was outside working in the garden. Please, come in!"

The Journalist walked in the door at the same time Tom walked down the stairway adjacent to the small foyer.

"Hey there," Tom said, extending his hand. "I see you've met my better half. It's great to see you again!"

Tom's wife excused herself, reminding Tom that she was going to need help later in the afternoon moving a shrub from one area of the yard to another. Tom assured her he wouldn't forget.

Tom directed the Journalist to a study off the living room. The smell of brewing coffee wafted through the air. Cheerful throw rugs accented dark hardwood floors, and a corner fireplace served as the focal point of the room. Tom beckoned to a couple of wingback chairs in front of a desk which faced the fireplace. All four walls were covered with book-laden shelves. Still more books sat expectantly in stacks on the floor around the furthermost chair.

"Please excuse the condition of my office." Tom smiled as he spoke. "This is the one area my wife leaves completely to me, but I guess that is pretty obvious." He clearly loved the comfortably cluttered room.

After they settled into the chairs holding the inevitable mugs of coffee, the Journalist shared his experiences at Community Church. He also explained a little of his past church encounters and questioned Tom about the differences at Community Church.

"I think there are a lot of things to consider," said Tom. "For one thing, we're not a congregation of perfect people, by any means, but I can tell you what I believe facilitated the atmosphere you experienced. The details of how it plays out practically are very different."

"Let's just begin at the beginning," suggested the Journalist.

"Well, several years ago, I asked our church leadership team to describe what they thought a Community Church member would look like if we were 100 percent successful in accomplishing our mission," said Tom. "I have come to call the process we went through the creation of a profile, or a picture of the ideal."

"And what did they say?" asked Journalist, leaning forward slightly.

"They first came up with a lot of words and descriptive phrases for this ideal member; words like caring, involved, in love with the Lord, able to share their faith in their world, having a distinctive Biblical world view – things like that."

"I asked our church leadership team to describe what they thought a Community Church member would look like if we were 100 per cent successful in accomplishing our mission."

"What happened next?"

"We took the list of descriptors and began to categorize them. We eventually wrote a paragraph that described what we would like to see our ideal church member look like. We called it the 'profile statement.'"

"And?" the Journalist prompted.

"Using this profile, I asked them to assess our current members, using a grading scale from A to D." Tom said. "I realized that what we were doing was somewhat subjective, but it provided us a basis for planning. Well, when it came right down to it, they graded our church members as a 'C,' pretty average from their standpoint. The next question I asked was why did you give them a 'C'?"

"What did they say?"

"They offered seven reasons, things like: 'we don't provide opportunities for people to exercise areas of personal giftedness,' and 'we don't have or provide a wide divergence of evangelistic opportunities that accommodate the places where our church members have influence.'" We listed them on a board and I asked them to rate them in order of their relative importance to the mission of our church."

"What happened then?"

"We began to plan," said Tom.

He put down his coffee mug on the corner of his desk and rubbed his hands together. Scooting slightly toward the edge of his chair, he warmed to his topic.

"The needs we identified guided me on the selection of topics that I would address in my sermons. We also used the 'ideal profile' as a yardstick to measure the curriculum we were using in our Sunday School and small groups. We went even further by making sure we provided opportunities to our members that would put them into environments which could help them address some of the broader issues we were committed to changing."

"Everything we do is planned with specific objectives in mind. In other words, we ask ourselves before every event or activity how we want a participant to walk away."

The Journalist was feverishly jotting notes on his legal pad. "What do you mean?" he asked, without looking up. "What kinds of things did you encourage people to participate in?"

"For example, we schedule two mission trips each year, one here in our country and one overseas. We participate in ministries at the local prison, at soup kitchens in the inner city, and minister practically to others in a variety of other venues. Everything we do is planned with specific objectives in mind. In other words, we ask ourselves before every event or activity how we want a participant to walk away."

"You mean, you 'profile' each activity, too." It was a statement, not a question.

"Precisely," Tom said, encouraged to see that the Journalist had been tracking the conversation well. "In fact, we profile everything around here. We profile what the perfect Sunday service would look like, what we want every Sunday School participant to look like at the end of each year, what every event we do would look like if it were totally successful in accomplishing its objective. Everything."

The Journalist stopped writing for a moment and stared into the dark, cool fireplace. Years of experience had caused him to conclude that success in most organizations catches them by surprise. Occasionally things happen, and the organization is genuinely pleased, but more often than not, they seemed shocked when success becomes apparent.

He broke from his reverie and spoke. "Do you use this planning tool in other ways?"

"...the fact that observable changes are occurring in our city as a result of the ministry of Community Church is not an accident."

"Yes – in fact it probably led to your visit in the first place," said Tom. "A magazine writer wrote a story about our church which captured the attention of your editor because it implied that Community Church was making a substantial difference in our city. Well let me tell you, the fact that observable changes are occurring in our city as a result of this ministry is not an accident. That same group of men and women answered another question I posed to them."

"Which was?"

"I asked them to look 10 years into the future, and then posed this question: 'How would our city be different one decade from now if we were successful in fulfilling our mission in the lives of people who chose to worship here?'"

Tom paused, allowing the words to sink in. The thought was profound at one level and unbelievably simple at another.

Finally the Journalist spoke. "I think I'm beginning to see."

Think About It . . .

1. What group of people within your church do you most easily relate?

2. Write a statement that reflects what you believe your group would look like if the work of the church was 100% successful in ministering to those in this group?

3. How would you grade the group right now, from A-D?

4. What are the deficiencies?

5. What could be done to address them?

6. Think about it.

⬧ *Chapter Nine*

Critical Groups

The Journalist felt the impact of their last meeting. He re-read the magazine article his editor first gave him, and things began to get clearer. The changes reported were not merely random successes, but a part of a clearly-strategized plan that Community Church developed to impact the city in ways consistent with its mission.

The very thought that a church leadership team would literally lay claim to the city seemed bold, even audacious. But Tom was like an evangelist, committed deeply to God and to impacting the world. It was as if he could see the changes as having already happened – changes in lives and changes in the culture. The idea was dynamic, but even better than that, it was a vision coming to reality.

"The changes that were being reported were not merely random successes, but part of a clearly-strategized plan that Community Church developed to impact the city in ways consistent with its mission."

Then there was the dynamism within the church. People were alive. They engaged with others – something the Journalist never before experienced. Most of his old friends 'checked out' when it came to others; living for themselves, pursuing their own selfish ambitions and not seeming to care who they hurt along the way. Life was a game to them, and winning was everything.

When the Journalist met with Tom the following day, he had even more questions. After exchanging pleasantries, he got right to the point.

"Do you remember me sharing my first impressions at Community Church?" he asked.

"I do," said Tom. "You spoke of feeling welcome, and I think the invitation to go to lunch with a group of our unmarried singles really impacted you. At least that's the way I remember it."

"You remember well," said the Journalist answered. "It's that group that I wanted to talk to you about. They are all involved in a Bible study together, and meet pretty regularly from what I can gather. They seem really engaged in one another's lives. What's behind all of that?"

Tom knew the Journalist had come to the point of no return – a hunger for God and the fellowship of His people was kindled. Journalistic curiosity may have been the impetus for the initial search, but the Holy Spirit had already made an impression on this earnest, seeking man, and nothing else would truly suffice.

He gestured toward the coffee maker in the corner of the room. "Want a refill before I launch into my thesis?" he said, smiling.

The Journalist returned the smile, but shook his head.

"Well, a number of years ago I sat down with our church leadership team and I asked them to identify groups within our church," said Tom. "I wanted them to write down as many groups of people as they could think of – college students, single parents, retired people, parents of college students, mothers of pre-school children, etc. They worked hard on the assignment and came up with about 40 different groups."

"I'm assuming one of the groups was the group that invited me to dinner that Sunday," the Journalist broke in..

"Probably," said Tom . "There were a lot of different groups. My next question was, 'In light of our vision to impact our city, can you place these groups into some kind of priority order?' I was looking to identify what I call 'critical groups,' as we prepared to launch some of our major planning initiatives."

"Like reaching the city for Christ?"

"Yes – that and other things we were trying to accomplish both in our community and within the church.

Tom paused for a moment, reflecting back on a time he obviously relished, then continued. "That first year we just selected 10 groups and began to focus on what we could do to facilitate the kind of results we wished to achieve, in terms of ministering effectively to members of those groups."

The Journalist chuckled. "What did you do? Let me guess, create a profile?"

"That's exactly what we did!" said Tom. "We sat down and prayed, asking the Lord for wisdom to understand the needs of individuals in each of these groups and identify what we might do to meaningfully address those needs. Then we asked ourselves this question; 'If we were impacting this group of people in ways consistent with the mission of our church, what would they look like if we were totally successful?'"

"And? What would a typical profile look like?"

"Well, for a group like the one which invited you to dinner, it might go something like this: 'Community Church is committed to providing an environment that facilitates spiritual growth so that individuals in this group can come to grips with

---

"We asked the question, 'if we were impacting this group of people in ways consistent to the mission of our church, what would they look like if we were totally successful?'"

---

their responsibilities as a disciple, a friend, a student of God's Word, and as a man or woman whom God created for His pleasure.'" Tom smiled. "That's just off the top of my head, but it might sound something like that."

"Not too bad for the top of your head," said the Journalist. "Now, what happened after you came up with this?"

"I asked our leadership team, 'if we could accomplish five things this year that might be used of the Lord in yielding these kinds of results, what five things would we do?'"

The Journalist leaned forward a little in anticipation. "Did you come up with five?" he asked.

"Yes we did. I can't recall exactly what we did in that year, but with a group like the one which invited you out, it might have been something like: (1) Seek to establish an accountability relationships among individuals within the group. (2) With the help of others, assist each individual within the group to identify an area of spiritual giftedness and work with them in determining how they might use that gift in service to God. (3) Participate in a group Bible study – something which could be done alone, but shared with one another. (4) Commit to meet with the group at least once each quarter. (5) Participate in a discipleship retreat sometime during the year."

"How did you keep the group on the same agenda?" The Journalist looked puzzled. "I mean, an accountability relationship might mean different things to different people."

"It might, and we understood that, so we 'profiled' again," said Tom. "We profiled each of the five objectives identified for that year and tried to paint a visual picture of what success would look like if each particular initiative was successfully accomplished."

"I should have known," replied the Journalist with a laugh. "But organizing all of this had to be a nightmare!"

"Actually, no," said Tom. He reached for a piece of paper and drew a circle. Inside the circle he drew two smaller circles. In the outside circle he drew some lines leaving about 25 individual blocks, in the center circle he created five blocks, and left the center circle empty.

"We profiled each of the five objectives identified for that year and tried to paint a visual picture of what success would look like if that initiative was successfully accomplished.

"This is a circle organizational chart," he explained. "In each of the blocks in the outside circle, we wrote a name of one of the individuals in the group. In each of the five blocks in the middle circle, we wrote the name of someone else. The center circle had the name of someone we selected to coordinate the activities of this group throughout the course of the year."

The Journalist did a quick mental calculation. "So this group has 31 people, right?"

"Right. In fact, if we had more than 25 people in a group, we just created another chart. Our team discovered that groups of 31 were about the maximum number we could work with and still be efficient in accomplishing strategic initiatives."

"Now what did these center circle people do?"

"The center circle person communicates regularly with his five middle circle support people. He meets with them about once a month. His purpose is to teach, inspire, equip and encourage this group to develop relationships with each of the five people in his own group."

"What would be some of the things these center circle people might do with those people in the outside circle?" asked the Journalist. He was intrigued by the unique organizational scheme.

"He would make sure that they had an accountability partner, initially, and then throughout the year he would check to see if they were meeting regularly, checking to see how things were going in the Bible study, inviting them to special events, things like that."

"But who teaches, inspires, equips, and encourages the center circle people?" The Journalist lifted his right hand from the legal pad and pointed to the large circle.

"We're not surprised when God accomplishes significant work in the lives of people – we expect it!"

"That's our job," said Tom. "I meet each month with about 10 different individuals. I pour my life into them. We dream together of what God could do in the lives of the group for which they are responsible, we pray for God's wisdom in helping us to understand individual needs, we think of creative ways to keep people engaged. Every member of our church staff has about 10 people as well. This year we have over 60 active circles. If you do the math that means that our church is pro-actively ministering to over 1,800 people!"

"Amazing!" exclaimed the Journalist. "Your ministry isn't arbitrary, it's intentional isn't it?"

"I discovered many years ago that there were many groups within churches who felt left out, and since the church wasn't impacting their lives in any meaningful way it was regarded as irrelevant. In some churches that might be single parents, in others, retired seniors or mothers of pre-schoolers. Obviously the lists could go on and on."

"I think I was in one of those groups," said the Journalist with a slight sigh. "Maybe that's why I gave up on church."

"The ministry of the church needs to touch the hearts of everyone!"

"Perhaps you were," Tom said. "The ministry of the church needs to touch the hearts of everyone. It's the only way we will be effective in accomplishing our God-ordained mission. That requires identifying every group we can imagine, determining before God how we desire to be used in their lives, assessing individual needs and then creating a plan with very specific objectives."

Then he added with a chuckle, "We also remind ourselves that we are simply facilitators, the results belong to God!"

"Yes," said the Journalist, nodding his acknowledgement. "And that's why you probably are seeing such tremendous impact in the lives of people. You aren't necessarily surprised when people start growing in Christ, are you?"

"No, we're not," said Tom. "We expect it."

Think About It . . .

1. List groups of people that exist within your church. Remember, often individuals will be a part of a number of groups.

2. Which group do you most readily relate?

3. Create a profile that describes what you perceive members of this group would look like if the mission of your church was 100% successful in ministering to them.

4. On an A-D scale (A is the highest), how would you rank your group?

5. Can you think of things that could happen this year in the lives of people that might bring them closer to this ideal? List some of them in the space provided.

6. Think about it.

Chapter Ten

A Church At Work

The Journalist found it difficult to fully grasp how Community Church could be so efficient in accomplishing its mission in the lives of so many people. It was enlightening to learn about the organizational structure the church utilized, but while it looked good on paper, the implementation of it still posed some questions he wanted answered.

As he re-read the notes from his last meeting with Tom he kept coming back to his initial conversation weeks before with Lynda. He reached for another legal pad and scanned its contents. Years of experience resulted in a note-taking scheme which enabled him to quickly pick up themes that surfaced during interviews. He glanced down the left hand side of the pad until he came to the word doctor.

In the right margin he had hastily written caring, empathic, genuine during his interview with Lynda. She used these words when describing the doctor at the hospital who had been the catalyst for her spiritual renewal.

He picked up the phone and punched out seven numbers.

"Hello, this is Lynda," was the reply after two rings. The lightness of her voice reminded him of their first phone conversation – which became the catalyst for his incredible journey.

"Hi, Lynda." The Journalist identified himself and then just blurted out, "I can't begin to tell you the impact our initial conversation had on me!"

"I've heard," she said. He could almost see the smile in her voice. "In fact the day you received God's gift of salvation through Christ I got a phone call from Tom. I couldn't be happier for you!"

She paused just a moment, then ventured, "Have you experienced any difference in your perspectives?"

It was a loaded question. The Journalist knew immediately that Lynda had a clear understanding of the situation.

"Difference?" he said, laughing. "More like a transformation! I mean there is hardly a comparison between now and then. The moment I left Tom's office that day a load was lifted, replaced by a peace I've never before known – a contented joy that sustains me despite the circumstances of the day. And that's only the beginning!"

"How wonderful!" she said. "I really understand what you're saying. For me, the day I received Christ was literally a life saver."

"I know," the Journalist replied, understanding the implications of her comment. "You know, Lynda, I was reviewing some notes earlier today and I was reminded of your story. You mentioned a doctor who really had an impact on your life."

"You mean Bill?" she said. "He is one of the leading urologists here in our hospital and one of the most incredible men I've ever met. Would you like to meet him sometime?"

"Interesting you should ask," he said. "That was really the purpose of my call. I've been spending a lot of time with Tom and he's explained some of the things that are happening at Community Church and the organizational structure behind them. I thought Bill might be able to give me the insight of another perspective."

"Well I don't know about that, but even if he couldn't answer some of your specific questions, it will still be a great meeting for you." Lynda was already clicking through her electronic address book.

Despite the doctor's busy schedule, Lynda put the two men in contact with one another and they agreed to meet for an early breakfast the next morning in the hospital cafeteria.

To identify himself, the Journalist simply said he looked like a newspaper man. When Bill arrived at the cafeteria, he spotted him right away.

"Good morning, I'm Bill," he approached the Journalist with an outstretched hand. "You wouldn't happen to be the newspaper man I'm looking for would you?"

"Is it that obvious?" the Journalist laughed. "I was hoping you might find the assignment of identifying me a little more challenging."

"Well the khakis, golf shirt, sneakers and legal pad were my first clue that you probably weren't an intern and since you are the only person standing here that I don't know I decided to take my chances." Bill smiled warmly as he put his hand on the back of the journalist guiding him toward the line.

Bill was a prominent and respected specialist in the city, but dressed in scrubs and sneakers, he blended in with the majority of those in the cafeteria. As they walked through the line he greeted everyone he saw by name, often asking them about families or commenting on some current issue.

Trays in hand, they walked to a table in a corner of the room.

"Gosh, it's good to see you," Bill turned his high wattage smile on the Journalist. "Lynda gave me a call yesterday and told me a little about you. I'm thrilled to learn that you have come to know Christ as your Savior. Do you mind telling me about it?"

"As they walked through the line he greeted everyone he saw by name and often asked them about their families or some issue he knew they were grappling with."

He seemed genuinely interested in learning more and time didn't seem a factor for the busy physician. His demeanor was relaxed, and bespoke a "bedside manner" which was undoubtedly a source of comfort to his patients.

The Journalist shared his story. In the interest of time he attempted to be brief, but was regularly pressed for details of the story. They laughed together frequently, and all the time Bill was attentive like he was with the most important person in the world.

Eventually, the Journalist tried to transition the conversation by asking, "You've had an impact on a lot of lives including Lynda's. Can you help me to understand more about that?"

"I'm not sure I totally understand the question," said Bill. "But let me begin by saying that for a lot of years I felt pretty unproductive in my spiritual life. I was radically changed when I received Christ and enthusiastic to share what had happened to me. Some people listened to me because they didn't feel like they had too much choice, but others ignored me, expressing happiness that I had found some answers to my questions about life but clearly indicating they wanted the conversation to end there."

"Is that still true?" the Journalist asked.

Bill smiled. "Yes, to some extent it is. What's changed, however, is I feel more productive because I've learned how to more effectively communicate my faith. I've come to realize that everyone is at a different place in their spiritual awareness and I seek to understand where that might be. I call them 'intersections,' moments in a person's life when they need to make choices. I just want to be there to have them to consider the possibility of Christ as an answer."

"But how do you do that?" The Journalist leaned forward with palpable interest.

"By asking questions," said Bill simply. "I've learned to be a better listener and ask probing questions in an effort to determine if God might be at work in their lives."

"I've learned to be a better listener and ask probing questions in an effort to determine if God might be at work in their lives."

"You can actually determine that?" asked the Journalist

"I believe so," was the solid reply.

Bill reached into the back pocket of his baggy scrubs and retrieved a small, taped-up copy of the New Testament. He flipped over to a passage in the book of Romans and read aloud, ""There is no one that seeks after God"".[1]

He looked up at the Journalist over the pages of the diminutive volume. "Don't you find that interesting?"

Not fully understanding where he was going, the Journalist replied, "Well I've seen many people who seem to be searching for something beyond themselves to address the troubling issues of life."

"I guess that's my point," Bill said. "That's the thing I'm seeking to find in people – whether they're searching for answers,

1. Romans 3:11

something beyond their ability to objectively cope. Salvation is totally of God. Only God can convict someone of sin and only God can initiate in a person the desire to seek Him. On our own, because of our sinfully depraved nature, we will never reach out to God."

The Journalist shook his head. "I guess I'm still missing the point."

"I'm anxious to know if God is at work in someone's heart," said Bill. "If He seems to be, I accept that as an invitation to share what Jesus has done in my life."

"But how do you determine if God is at work?" Again, the Journalist leaned forward, nearly getting syrup on his shirt.

"By asking questions!" Bill exclaimed, grinning like he'd just delivered the grand prize. "I like to listen – to learn who people are, what's happening in their lives, the questions they have and the really big issues they're grappling with. And as I listen, they might express conviction over something or a desire to learn more about God, or just a desire to make some sense out of the chaos in their lives."

"I just like to listen and to learn where people are, what is happening in their lives, the questions about life that they have, and the really big issues with which they are grappling."

Understanding broke over the Journalist's face. "So, if they indicate something that God says only He can do, then you know to introduce Him into the conversation, right?"

"Exactly!" Bill emphatically smacked the table top. His plastic fork went flying off the table, and he chuckled as he bent to retrieve it.

"It's still important to be sensitive," he added, sitting back up. "Rather than tell them what I believe the answer to their questions or concerns are, I suggest that they might want to think about a particular thought or read something that I feel might be especially relevant. I might share that I had the same concerns at one time in my life and found the answer in a personal relationship with Christ."

"And then?"

"I might even ask if I can pray for them, right there. And I will always follow up with a phone call, or make a point to look them up within the next day or two. I do that with some level of confidence because I know that God's at work in their hearts. I just quietly, hopefully tactfully, and lovingly pursue them in the same spirit God pursued me."

"And with some success, I can assure you," the Journalist added. "Lynda's life was dramatically changed by Christ and she is quick to share that your life and example had a tremendous impact in drawing her to the Lord."

Bill smiled and waved both hands in front. "It's all about God – He just uses people like you and me. Go figure, we're a pretty motley group when you get right down to it."

The Journalist enjoyed this man. Unpretentious and ordinary as the guy next door, he made his faith 'approachable.'

"Bill, do you ever feel all alone out here?" he asked. "I mean, it can be lonely when you feel nobody really cares about the things that are really important to you."

"Community Church is committed to being intentional in ministry."

"Oh, no – I'm part of a group of men at Community Church who have committed themselves to one another," said Bill. "We meet regularly to study together, pray together, pray for one another, and hold ourselves spiritually accountable to one another. It's fantastic. I've never felt alone."

The Journalist nodded. "Tom's been telling me about these groups. I understand that there are many of them operating within Community Church."

"I don't know the exact number but just about everybody I know is in at least one group," said Bill. "They're very informal, but there's a clearly defined agenda for each year and we really work to create an environment within the group which facilitates the spiritual changes we want to see evidenced in our lives."

There it was again: relationships. It all went back to relationships. The Journalist recalled all Tom said about their importance, and how they provide the context in which all meaningful change occurs.

"Community Church is committed to being intentional in ministry," continued Bill. "There's a belief that we can create an environment for change, and to do that we must be pro-active in pursuing people. We must not assume that just because we say something, everyone can figure it out on their own and know what to do with it."

"Seems like I've heard that before," the Journalist replied.

Think About It . . .

1. If your church was to reach out to claim your community for Christ, what groups exist within your community that you would want to initially focus upon?

2. Can you think of "entry level" opportunities that you might provide to expose them to Christ?

3. Are there people in your church who are already a part of these groups and who might be used of the Lord in reaching out to the group of which they are already a part?

4. Think About It.

Chapter Eleven

Outreach

The Journalist reviewed what he'd learned, impressed by the amount of planning behind the scenes at Community Church. Tom's vision was clear: a congregation committed to building relationships so that gifted, equipped and changed people could go into their world, reflecting the image of Christ.

Even more amazing was that the real work of change taking place in the city was not accomplished by people on the payroll – rather they were church members with jobs, families and other responsibilities. Tom often reiterated that serving God 'isn't a vocation, it's a way of life.' The Journalist could see evidence of that in Lynda, in the life of Bill who had impacted her life so dramatically, even in the lives of the group who invited him to dinner one Sunday afternoon.

"Serving God isn't simply a vocation, it's a way of life."

He never forgot his first visit with Lynda. As he grew to understand more of what was happening within the church, he was sure that there was a similar strategy in place to reach the city – that there was more to Lynda's experience than met the eye. He really wanted to know the role that Community Church played in creating the event that led to Lynda's conversion to Christ.

The Journalist called Tom again and requested another meeting.

"Why don't we meet at the coffee shop," said Tom.

"When would be good for you," asked the Journalist.

Tom suggested meeting in 15 minutes, but then added, "Hey listen, if you buy the coffee I can be there in ten!"

"Deal! I'm racing to the car right now."

A few minutes later they sat in overstuffed chairs, lattés in hand.

"I'm so glad you called," said Tom, after a creamy sip. "I just finished some work and was looking for an excuse to get out of the office!"

"Glad to be of service," said the Journalist with a wry smile.

Then, anxious to begin the discussion, he bypassed further small talk.

"You might remember that Lynda was my first exposure to someone involved in Community Church. She totally threw me for a loop. I mean, she was open, honest, sweet and very committed to her faith. She told me about some things that were happening in the medical community and how those activities were instrumental in bringing her to faith in Christ."

"Yes, I think that's true," said Tom expecting the follow up question.

"I bet you can tell me exactly what was going on, and I'm sure it wasn't circumstantial!"

"You're a quick learner!" Tom said, and they both laughed.

"We take the job of sharing the good news – the gospel – very seriously. And we've learned that there are things that people do to indicate whether or not God is at work in their lives. We have clearly thought through all of that and developed clearly defined strategies to reach people groups within the city where we live."

"I'm all ears."

Tom took a pen from his shirt pocket and drew a picture on his napkin. A wavy line near the bottom represented waves of the sea. Under this, he wrote the words, 'Sea of Prospects.' Inside the wavy lines he drew a few fish.

"This is intended to represent a sea in which there is every resource we would ever need to accomplish the mission God gave us. All the prayer partners we'll ever need are in the Sea of Prospects, all the volunteers are in the sea, all the giftedness we would require to do our work is in the sea . . . it's limitless."

He continued with his drawing, placing an island in the middle of the sea. Atop the island he drew a crude stick house.

"You better stick with your day job," the Journalist joked.

Tom examined his drawing. "I think you're right! You may

have to exercise a little faith in the interpretation of my artwork here."

The Journalist squinted comically. "Okay, ready."

"Now, this little house with its front door and front porch represents Community Church. Many good things happen here in this place. God is actively at work in the lives of hundreds of people, and change is taking place – significant change."

"I would agree," said the Journalist.

"The problem is there are many people down here," pointing to the sea, "in the Sea of Prospects we long to reach, but the vast majority have never been in this house," said Tom, pointing to the crude house drawing. "Some of them might not even know it exits. Therein lays the great challenge of ministry: How can our church be used of God to reach these people?"

Tom paused and looked pointedly at the Journalist, caught in mid-sip.

"Invite them to come by?" he suggested meekly, wiping his mouth with the back of his hand.

---

*". . . (in the Sea of Prospects) is every resource
we would ever need to accomplish
the mission which God gave us!"*

"There you go again!" Tom beamed. "You're absolutely right!"

He drew an arrow from the Sea of Prospects to the front porch of the house. "I call this the 'Entry Level Opportunity'. It's the various opportunities we provide to introduce people to our church and its various outreach ministries."

"You mean like the church-sponsored medical symposiums for the hospital personnel?"

"Yes, exactly" said Tom.

He pointed back to his drawing, tapping the porch. "Sometimes people come to our church and stand right here on the front porch – and sometimes we take the front porch to them, as with the medical symposiums. In either case, they are now in a position to get a peek of what's inside the house."

"Kind of like what happened to Lynda, right?"

"Precisely," said Tom. "The medical seminars represented a vision Bill had that he thought might enable him to connect with those he knew and with whom he worked. He knows a great number of health care professionals and initially began inviting people over to his home. He just shared some thoughts on topics of interest to him and them but also shared Christ as a meaningful alternative to some of the deeply rooted questions people in his profession need to address."

The Journalist took a moment to digest what Tom said. Then, speaking slowly as if continuing to process his thoughts, he asked, "When you talk about getting a peek inside, what exactly did you mean?"

"Each participant learns something important at these seminars. They also experience people and have a chance to observe what makes them 'tick.' Such is the case with Bill– he lives such an incredible testimony in front of people, it just arouses curiosity. People can't understand how he can be upbeat at times when there's no practical reason."

"Yes, Lynda said as much." The Journalist took a long, thoughtful sip on his cooling latté.

"But if it all ended at the end of the seminar, Lynda might still be lost and without Christ," said Tom. "Think of this, if you came to my house and walked up to my door and knocked, I would open the door and greet you. What do you think the next thing I would do?"

"Probably invite me in."

"Exactly, and that's what we try to do every time we bring people to the front porch – we invite them in!"

Tom placed his empty coffee cup on the table and gestured emphatically with both hands. "It might be expressed in ways like, 'If this is something that intrigues you, then let me share with you a couple of different ways you could plug into more events just like this.' The presenter might share five or six ways to get involved."

"That's exactly what happened to Lynda!" The Journalist remembered Lynda's recounting of the invitation that had been extended to her.

"I think people make two wrong assumptions in dealing with others," Tom went on with his explanation. "One is that when you say something, everybody gets it, and my experience is that's simply not true."

"I'm sure any parent of a teenager could verify that," interjected the Journalist with a chuckle.

"The other wrong assumption we make is that even if people do 'get it,' you cannot assume they know what to do with it, or will take the initiative to find out."

The Journalist nodded vigorously. "I've heard lots of things over the years and still don't know what to do with them, uh, like trigonometry, for example."

"I never got that either," Tom said, smiling. "Now, I call the invitation to come in 'The Bridge.' The Bridge is formed by things we suggest which take someone from the front porch into the foyer – you know, an invitation, something to which you have to say 'yes' or 'no.'"

"Bridging, extending that invitation to come inside, is the most important step in the procedure and we have made a commitment to bridge absolutely everything we do."

"Like you did this past Sunday?" Comprehension dawned across the face of the Journalist. "At the end of the service you said, 'Here are five things you can do this week to take the truth of God's Word and apply it in your world.' I remember that and believed there were two things I could use immediately. Is that what you mean by a bridge?"

"That's exactly what I mean," Tom replied. "You see, the challenge we face is to discern what kind of Entry Level Opportunities we can create to expose people to the good news of God's love. In the case of Bill, he chose to do something in an area where he is particularly gifted, presenting special seminars which address issues of critical concern to people in his profession."

"I'm beginning to see," said the Journalist. "So part of the strategy to reach people is to identify the groups of which they are a part, determine possibilities for Entry Level Opportunities and then invite them to come to the front porch so they can get a view of life from a different perspective."

"You've got it!" Tom exclaimed. "But you don't want to leave them on the front porch. If God has touched them there, imagine what could happen if they were inside! That's where The Bridge comes in. I have come to the conclusion that most organizations bring hundreds, if not thousands, of people to the front porch but then leave them there. Bridging, or extending that invitation to come inside, is the most important step in the procedure. We made a commitment to bridge absolutely everything we do."

The Journalist had been making doodles on his notepad. Now as he stared down at his drawing, he asked, "There is always more than one bridge, right?"

"We provide as many bridges as we can – remember, our goal is to get people into the foyer! Our desire is to give them as many opportunities as we can to say 'yes' to our invitation because it's in the house that we can really see the impact of ministry taking root in their hearts. And while it's true that everyone might not respond to the invitation to come in, you've got to remember that no one would come in if an invitation wasn't extended."

The Journalist nodded silently while he wrote a few more notes. He looked up. "Okay, I think I'm actually getting this. You creatively look for various ways to expose people to ministry by creating different entry level and front porch opportunities. Once there, you give them the opportunity to see what's inside and then extend the invitation to come in."

"Right," said Tom. "And while some may not choose to pursue the relationship any further, others might be searching for answers. We want to do what we can to help!"

Think About It . . .

1. Think of the (critical) group of which you are a part. What kinds of opportunities would you respond to that might be designed to bring you to "the front porch?"

2. What kinds of bridges could you imagine someone offering that might cause you to respond by "coming into the house?"

3. What group are you a part of vocationally? Repeat the exercises 1 and 2 above as it relates to this group. Are you willing to be involved in reaching them?

4. Think About It.

※ *Chapter Twelve*

A Church Triumphant

Attendance at Community Church was becoming a much anticipated habit with the Journalist. The dread in which he anticipated church as a child was replaced with an enthusiasm to be with others, to study the Bible, and learn more how to utilize his gifts in making a difference where he lived.

There was also the distinct aura of love – not necessarily expressed in big toothy smiles or bear hugs all around – but present nonetheless. It seemed like the natural emanation of the people who worshipped there.

On a prominent wall in the foyer, the mission of Community Church was boldly written: "Community Church is committed to providing an environment that draws people to an intimate, personal relationship with Jesus Christ, an atmosphere that

---

Everyone he met over the months had clear direction and seemed to understand his or her role in accomplishing the vision of ministry."

---

would foster building relationships with one another, and a variety of opportunities where those who have been redeemed can be trained and equipped to fulfill the mandate of His Church to the community and to the world."

The Journalist had seen first hand the ways in which this church was fulfilling that mission. Over the course of their many meetings, Tom had explained how the church leadership team carefully profiled each component of the mission, emphasizing the diligence with which they created and pursued a plan to fulfill their corporate calling.

Everyone he met over the months had clear direction and seemed to understand his or her role in accomplishing this vision of ministry. They also seemed to understand individual giftedness and felt comfortable in the various ways they served God. Bankers, accountants, single moms, lawyers, teenagers, families, senior citizens and dozens of other groups worked alongside each other, utilizing their unique gifts to fulfill this mission among those with whom they worked and lived.

People throughout the city were receiving the gift of God's love in Christ. And as church members facilitated change through their efforts, they also experienced transformation in their lives.

Most amazing of all, there began to be discernable differences in the culture of the city.

The Journalist attended forums led by church members, read the stories of people transformed in the church newsletter, reviewed articles appearing in professional journals that had been penned by church members, observed the impact of church members who served on community boards and followed the many stories of others who felt called to serve their Savior in the inner city, in nursing homes, prisons, building homes, and scores of other venues.

He became aware of major improvements in education, had learned of many cooperative efforts that engaged the races in addressing community needs, had evaluated statistics that reported an increasing level of volunteerism among people who lived in the community, and was privy to programs and projects initiated by individuals and churches to address vital issues of community concern. The culture of the community was slowly changing and behind the scenes their were people, many of whom were associated with churches like Community Church, who weren't leaving the issues for someone else to resolve but who chose to be involved in presenting a spiritual dimension to some of the regions most troubling problems.

He also learned more about what was happening internally at Community Church; the work that Tom called the "training and equipping" of those within the church to do the work of ministry. He discovered that the key to building relationships at Community Church revolved around critical groups and discovered all the creative ways in which these groups were organized and what was being accomplished each year in the lives of literally hundreds of church members. In addition, a network of small groups had also been established where training occurred and ministry initiatives launched.

He became part of a critical group of thirty young professionals. Using a specially-designed study guide, they set about the task of defining a Biblical world view and personally assessing how that world view should affect their responses to every aspect of contemporary culture. He noticed that other critical groups studied topics unique to them. Most groups met formally once a quarter, but interacted continually on a social and professional level.

"Success ought not to be a surprise, rather it is the combination of two vital ingredients: a clearly defined plan and total dependence upon God."

Tom called it "the church intentional." He reminded the Journalist over and over again that success ought not to be a surprise, rather it is the combination of two vital ingredients: a clearly defined plan and total dependence upon God.

The mission of Community Church was to miss no one; to make sure everyone knew they had a role and a responsibility to Christ to reach the world with the message of His redeeming love – one community, one person at a time.

This was a church that knew its mission and pursued it with passion like he had never seen. It was a church that was making a difference.

Think About It . . .

1. How do you think your community would be different if your church were 100% successful in accomplishing its mission?

2. How could you imagine the local culture might change?

3. Are you willing to take the risk and reach out to others for the cause of Christ?

4. Think About It.

The Conclusion

The article appeared over three pages in the city newspaper, with the bold headline: "Making a Difference One Life at a Time."

The in-depth feature reported the activities of professional men and women, families, seniors, teens and others who took their faith to their world. It emphasized the changes attributed to their work – both locally and nationally.

Response to the article was enormous. Churches throughout the city, the country and the world began to follow the lead of ministry practiced at Community Church.

Two years later, a cover story appeared in a national news magazine. The cover picture showed the earth as seen from space and the title caption read, "A Planet Revived." The article detailed the story of worldwide spiritual revival and reported the stories of countries transformed by God.

The lead article, entitled, "A World Changed Through Relationships," focused on one relationship – that between God and the millions who fulfilled their commission to Him to their generation.

A tiny byline appeared at the end of the story. The name was that of The Journalist.

Appendices

The Church Intentional

Transforming Culture: The Church at Work in the World speaks to the issue of intentionality in the way in which The Church fulfills its mission.

Success too often catches most churches by surprise. Occasionally someone will be impacted in a very significant way by our work and we are quick to share their story with others. We may speak of the changes that have occurred, even encourage the one who has changed to share their story with others as we stand gratified alongside at what has been accomplished through our ministry. But too often while this story is being told there are hundreds of other stories that are untold, stories of people like The Journalist who left the church as a teenager finding its message and mission irrelevant.

In chapter nine The Journalist becomes intrigued by the strategies of Community Church to impact critical groups of people within the congregation. The story relates how the church organized itself to pro-actively minister to individuals within each of these groups and how the church leadership focused their attention on inspiring, equipping, and training the recruited leaders of each group. The process so intrigued the Journalist that he exclaimed, "Your ministry isn't arbitrary, it's intentional, isn't it?" Later in the book Tom describes Community Church as "the church intentional."

Imagine the difference a local church could make if it became more intentional in its ministry to people within the congregation and in its outreach ministry to the community where it is located. Rather than hope for results wouldn't it be wonderful if we could say with the same level of confidence exuded by Tom when he responded to the Journalist's question "You aren't necessarily surprised when people start growing in Christ are you?" with these words, "No, we're not. We expect it."

Transforming Culture describes the implementation of a number of developmental "models" within the context of a local church. These models, along with some important definitions, rules and other concepts, are developed in greater detail in the following pages. "Transforming Culture" seminars are conducted throughout the world and special TC Software enables organizations to track emerging relationships within the ministry environment.

For more information about other Transforming Culture tools, please check out the website:
www.transformingculture.org.

The Attitude Continuum

The introduction of the book explains the steps which lead to an attitude of cynicism in the Journalist. Attitudes determine to a significant degree what impact ministry initiatives might have on peoples' lives.

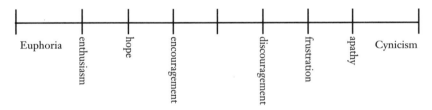

The line above illustrates the wide range of attitudes held by individuals in relationships, or an attitude continuum. These attitudes generally reflect how people perceive life as well as their attitudes toward the relationships in their lives, (e.g. relationships with spouses, churches and other organizations). Every individual can find themselves somewhere on this line as they rate themselves in terms of their important relationships.

Assuming the middle of the line reflects a neutral position (a point where someone has not committed themselves attitudinally to a relationship), there are three steps which lead to either cynicism or euphoria.

Three Steps to Cynicism

Steps leading to cynicism are:

• **Discouragement**—Something typically occurs within the

relationship that is unexpected and not in accordance with personal expectations.

- **Frustration**—Failing to deal with discouragement results in frustration. In the case of the Journalist, his exasperation increased as people continued to ignore the desperate needs of others.
- **Apathy**—Constant frustration develops into apathy – indifference as to whether the discouraging situation will ever be resolved.
- **Cynicism**—Cynicism is apathy unchecked. It's harder and more coarse; more than an attitude, it's often perceived by others as a way of life.

Three Steps to Euphoria

On the positive side, there are discernable steps which lead to unbridled enthusiasm:

- **Encouragement**—Something typically occurs within the relationship that gives reason to be encouraged.
- **Hope**—Continued encouragement brings hope. At this stage, individuals in relationship allow themselves to believe their expectations might, in fact, be realized.
- **Enthusiasm**—As hope grows, so does enthusiasm. There is a positive belief that things are moving in a very positive direction, and this will result in the realization of expectations.
- **Euphoria**—When things continue to move forward and the expectations of relationship are realized, euphoria results.

Two Important Facts

Everyone is somewhere on the attitude continuum as it relates to their relationships. Where individuals find themselves on the attitude continuum reflects their perceptions of an entity's ability to accomplish those expectations. For example, someone with a cynical attitude toward the church probably had expectations which were not met. If someone is cynical about marriage, they probably experienced a reality that was different from what they imagined.

Another factor of significance is that organizations (and individuals) cannot absolve themselves of responsibility when it comes to the attitudes held by others; after all, they are the ones who create an environment of expectation among those to whom they minister. Plans stated that are not practically achievable only exacerbate the problem by creating negative attitudes among the very people who are essential for taking the organization to its goal.

The Journalist and Change

Something had to occur in the life of the Journalist to move him from where he was attitudinally to a point where he could be more effective in accomplishing his life goals. This obviously occurs in the positive experiences he has with individuals associated with Community Church.

Important Definitions

Transforming Culture is about organizational and ministry development, a process that all organizations utilize in seeking to accomplish their stated missions. The story incorporates the application of certain principles drawn from a model of development known as "relational development."

To understand this model, it is essential to understand its two driving definitions:

- **Development**—represents the things an organization does to build rational relationships with others.
- **Successful Development**—measured in terms of an organization's ability to sustain the involvement of constituents.
  The ability to "transform" lives can be measured in terms of how effectively these objectives are accomplished.

Development

Development is all about relationships. It has very little to do with money, despite the fact that most organizational development programs are focused on securing cash. It has very little to do with size, influence and impact which (ironically) becomes the primary objectives of many organizations and ministries.

In actuality, an organization or ministry that is successful in building relationships never lacks for money. Money, size, influence and impact are the result of building relationships! But if we lead with our "needs" at the expense of building enduring relationships, we are often perceived as manipulative.

Rational relationship implies that the sustained involvement of people to one another and to an organization (such as their church) is based on commitment. While emotion might draw people together in relationship, it is rationalism that keeps them together. The mission statement of an organization is the basis of rationality. In the context of Community Church, people understood the church mission. It was that mutual commitment to the mission which drew people together and kept them persistently reaching out to others.

Successful Development

Success in development activities is evidenced by sustainability. In the context of organizations such as churches, sustainability can be measured by attrition percentages. For example, churches who lose members regularly are not "developmentally successful." If attrition becomes an issue, it is prudent to question the factors which precipitated it.

Four Things That Determine Development Success

There are four essential elements to success in development. They are best depicted by looking at a triangle:

- **Mission**—At the base of the triangle is mission. Mission is everything to successful development. It is the essence of rationality, reflecting in each of its phrases the very heart of what the organization is committed to accomplish. Everything that happens within an organization needs to be driven by the underlying mission.
- **Vision**—At the peak of the triangle is the vision of an organization. Vision might be defined as "mission accomplished." At various times in the book, Transforming Culture, this question is raised: "What would this group of people look like if the church was 100 percent successful in accomplishing its mission in their lives?" The description of that ideal represents the vision for that particular ministry.
- **The Strategic Plan**—The left side of the triangle reflects the process that must occur to bring an organization (church)

from where it is, to where it intends to go (vision). It might look like a series of steps – each representing one year – with specific quantifiable goals which must occur to move the organization toward its goal.

- **The Development Plan**—The diagram is completed only when the corresponding stairway on the opposite side reflects a plan which will provide all the resources (money, time, people) required to achieve the goals within the allocated time frame.

Special attention is needed for making certain that each dimension of this model is in place. The more secure the model, the more successful the development.

Three Reasons Why People Sustain Their Support of a Ministry

Individuals sustain their support of ministry for three primary reasons:

- **Mission**—They know your mission. It is important that people know the reasons for your existence and how you intend to accomplish your goals.
- **Belief**—Not only do they need to know the mission, but sustained supporters also believe in the importance of that mission.
- **Confidence**—Supporters pour resources into a ministry to the extent they have confidence in its ability to accomplish its goals.

The Procedure of Engaging People

Another model described in Transforming Culture is the procedure Community Church utilized for outreach. This model included internal efforts to impact members of the congregation and external efforts to reach others in the community with the redemptive message of God's love.

The diagram that best reflects this procedure was described by Tom as an island in the middle of a vast sea. On the island is a house that represents the ministry.

The sea is called the Sea of Prospects. Within the sea is virtually every resource the church needs to accomplish its mission:

prayer partners, volunteers, resources, etc

The house (ministry) is attractive. It has a front door and a front porch. Great things are accomplished in the house – lives are transformed, like the life of the Journalist. What happens in his life was only reflective of what happened earlier in the lives of others (Lynda, Bill, etc.).

The challenge is to match up the resources in the Sea of Prospects with the ministry on the hill.

The Three Steps

The procedure to meet that challenge involves three steps, first described in the story Lynda relates to the Journalist:

- **The Entry Level Opportunity**—This is an opportunity for people in the Sea of Prospects to come to the front porch of the house. In the case of Lynda, that opportunity was a special seminar offered as an outreach ministry of Community Church to the medical community. Entry level opportunities bring people to the "front porch" where the "front door" is opened for individuals to get a glimpse of what is inside.
- **The Bridges**—This step is the one most frequently ignored in the execution of development. Bridges are invitations or opportunities to which people may respond with either a "yes" or a "no." These answers are rational decisions and become the basis of any long-term relationship. In Lynda's case, several opportunities were provided after the seminar for other activities of a similar nature, communications about future events, etc.
- **Conversion**—The result of a successful bridge is (in development terms) a conversion. For example, if 100 people came to the seminar Lynda attended and 50 of them expressed an interest in learning more, that is a 50 percent conversion rate. Conversion percentages should be tracked by all ministries in conjunction with development activities.

Two Characteristics of Relationships

Transforming Culture is a story of how the Lord used relationships to transform lives as well as culture. All aspects of the church's calling are enhanced in the context of relationships, and there are two ingredients common to all relationships:

- **Choice**—People make choices to move into relationships. Not everyone chooses to be in relationship with another. Few will choose to move into relationship without an invitation or opportunity to do so. Extending that invitation is a critical step in the relationship-building process.
- **Sacrifice**—Every successful relationship requires sacrifice from both participants. The bridges in the procedural model described here provide people with the opportunity to make choices and the subsequent sacrifices if they choose to accept the invitation to relationship.

Two Wrong Assumptions in Ministry

Tom, the pastor of Community Church, recognized two assumptions in ministry that are often wrongfully made. These are:

- **Everyone "Gets It"**—We can't assume that just because something is said aloud, that everyone who heard it totally understands it. Some may have a greater comprehension than others, but if ministry is to be effective, it is better to assume that the full impact of your communication was not understood.
- **Everyone Knows What To Do Next**—It is equally wrong to assume that people know exactly what to do with information they receive. Most individuals won't take the initiative to figure out the next steps. This developmental model suggests steps to next consider.

Important Reminders

The goal of ministry development is to impact the lives of people. People not only need exposure to our message and ministry, they also need an invitation inside the "house" where true relationships can be established. As these steps are implemented it is important to remember certain rules:

- **Provide Multiple Bridges**—Allow people the opportunity to consider opportunities with varying degrees of commitment. Remember the ultimate goal of this step in the development process is to move people into the house where relationship building occurs. In the case of the medical seminar that Lynda attended, after the event was over someone stood up and presented a number of "bridges" to which all participants were encouraged to consider. Tom also used "bridges" in his sermons to show how people could take the message and apply it immediately in areas where they lived and worked.

- **Keep the Threshold Low**—You want people in the house! Don't make the threshold so high that no one will choose to step inside. In the case of Lynda, there were several non-threatening opportunities to which she could respond after the seminar. Her affirmative response signaled she had more than just a passing interest in the programs offered by Community Church.

As church ministries reach out to others (especially to those outside the community of faith), they should make certain that when people come to their front porch they are always invited inside!

The Planning Model

Much of the story of how Community Church engaged others revolves around a "planning model" which defines the initiatives used to engage others in meaningful and life-changing relationships.

Planning is essential to successful ministry. While many churches and ministries have a vision that reflects their long-term goals, relatively few have a plan to get there. Statistics indicated that only 12 percent of churches and ministries have a strategic plan that demonstrates quantifiable steps which will move the organization from where it is to where it intends to go. Any "plan" that lacks quantification is merely a "good idea" that will likely never be achieved.

The Planning Model utilized by Community Church has eight basic steps. Understanding each of these steps is essential to the effective implementation of the model:

- **The Profile**—This is a description of the ideal. We see the profiling process several times in Transforming Culture. The question profiling answers is: "If we were 100 percent successful in accomplishing our mission in this area of ministry, what would the result look like?" Effective planning begins with the intended result and then backs into the steps that accomplish the desired results.

- **Assessment**—Once the result (goal) is established in a profile, that profile needs to be laid alongside reality. Community Church had to answer the question, "How does reality measure up to our ideal?" An effective way to assess is to give a grade from A-D. What letter adequately reflects where you are? An "A" would represent the fact that you match the ideal perfectly, a "B" might indicate that you match the profile in many ways, a "C" would reflect the fact that there are some ways in which the profile is being met, and a "D" would indicate that there's a way to go!

- **Quantification**—This step in the planning model answers the question, "Why?" Why did you give yourself the grade that you did? This step requires that you spell out the deficiencies between the profile and reality.

- **Prioritization**—Of all the areas listed as deficiencies, which are the most "mission critical" as it relates to your ministry? In most cases, it is impossible to address all the issues in any given planning period. Prioritization will enable you to identify the most crucial issues for achieving your vision.

- **Planning**—Planning cannot occur apart for the previous four steps. As stated earlier, any plan lacking quantification isn't a plan, it's a good idea! A plan lays out the steps which will move your vision forward in a particular area of the planning profile. Each step needs to be clear, measurable and assessed regularly.

- **Organization**—Once a plan is in place, an organizational infrastructure must accommodate the intended results. Community Church created a variety of small groups and each group had specific objectives to accomplish within the context of relationship. These objectives were clear – everyone knew what they were – and the groups regularly "measured" to determine whether they were making progress. The church also launched outreach initiatives in which they utilized similar organizational tactics to achieve their goals of bringing the message of God's redeeming love to certain community segments.

- **Implementation**—Once all things are in place, execution of the plan begins. Community Church was alive with scores of small groups meeting regularly and many more "outreach" initiatives taking place to reach identified critical groups within the community.

- **Evaluation**—The final step in the planning process takes place through regular and thoughtful evaluation. The question "How well did the plan work?" needs to be answered along with "Are there ways in which we can improve our plan to have even greater impact in achieving our vision?"

This eight stop process is articulated in greater detail in The Organizational Planning Primer, a workbook available at www.transformingculture.org.

The Organizational Model

The final model Community Church effectively utilized for ministry to its members and community outreach was an organizational model. Tom described it to the Journalist as three circles that looked something like this:

Circle Organization

The structure is designed to implement an intended plan. Before an organizational chart can be completed, it is important to note the following:

- **The Outer Circle**—This represents the individuals and/or initiative components which are the focus of the plan. In the case of Community Church, the names of individuals who composed a "critical group" were listed in the outside circle. For maximum effectiveness, there should be no more than 25 names in this outer circle.
- **The Middle Circle**—The middle circle includes the names of individuals who assume some responsibility for making sure key ministry objectives are accomplished in the lives of the critical group (the outer circle).
- **The Center Circle**—One name in the center assumes responsibility for coordinating activities within this circle. This individual communicates with middle circle people to

ensure all required resources are received, understood and addressed by those in the outer circle.

Planning Initiatives

Not every need of a critical group will be realized in one planning period (approximately nine months). When planning key initiatives at any level, it is important to keep in mind the following:

- **Five Objectives**—An organization should narrow down its planning objectives to five for any given planning period. This requires prioritizing needs and focusing on how to address the top five through a carefully constructed plan.
- **Planning**—Any model requires planning. Each of the five objectives should be carefully planned, utilizing the model described earlier on pages 105-107. Here is what the question needs to ask, "If we were 100 percent successful in accomplishing this ministry objective, what would it look like?"
- **Accountability**—The organizational model makes room for accountability. The center circle coordinates, equips and inspires those in the middle circle, and the middle circle people deliver key initiatives to those in the outside circle.
- **Manageability**—This organizational chart makes large initiatives manageable. The center circle coordinators are accountable to a member of the church leadership team who works with them in planning, dreaming, praying and equipping them for their assigned work.

Transforming Culture Tools

To support the Transforming Culture commitment of thousands of churches throughout the world, a special series of resources are readily available:

- **Transforming Culture Seminars**—Special "Transforming Culture" one-day seminars are scheduled around the world. Check out the schedule of seminars at: www.transformingculture.org. Using the website, you may also request a seminar in your area.
- **Transforming Culture Software**—A church software pro-

gram which accommodates all aspects of the Transforming Culture program, as well as many other church development tools, is available at www.transformingculture.org. This software provides invaluable help for identifying critical groups, planning key initiatives, implementing organization and tracking impact.

- **Pocket Precepts**—Churches committed to reaching their communities (cities) for Christ may use a specially created series of Critical Group Bible Studies, designed to take no more than 30 minutes a week to complete and typically run 16-24 weeks in length. Our website provides titles currently available for use within commonly identified critical groups.
- **Workbooks**—A series of workbooks are available to churches and ministries participating in the Transforming Culture program. Congregations are urged to purchase the study guide for this book available at our website.
- **Certification Program**—A professional certification program is available for individuals within churches and ministries who choose to be certified as a Transforming Culture coordinator. In addition to professional certification, one-day training programs for participating churches in the Transforming Culture program are held regularly throughout the world.
- **Covenant**—It is our prayer than 250,000 churches around the world will take the challenge of "claiming their communities" for Christ. A covenant is included as a part of this book that can be signed and sent to Transforming Culture, 6830 Fox Lake N. Drive, Indianapolis, IN 46278 or faxed to: 317/872-5412. Your church will be listed on the Transforming Culture website and will be encouraged to join together with another church somewhere else in the world in encouragement and support.
- **Stories**—If you have stories to tell of how your church has impacted your community for Christ, please tell your story in a section reserved for reports on the Transforming Culture website. The impact of your congregation's outreach will be an encouragement to others.

Transforming Culture Covenant

Believing that _____ *(Church, Ministry, or Individual Name) is part of the universal Church of Jesus Christ, the organism through which God has chosen to bear testimony of the redemptive work of His Son, Jesus Christ in the world in which we live and believing that:*

- **Our Lord commanded His disciples go into all the world with the message of the gospel (Matthew 28:19-20),**
- **That He left this earth admonishing His disciples to be witnesses in Jerusalem, Judea, Samaria and the uttermost parts of the earth (Acts 1:8),**
- **That He has uniquely gifted His children to serve through providing individual spiritual gifts (Romans 12, 1 Corinthians 12),**
- **That He has established His Church, the "body of Christ" to train and equip the redeemed for the work of ministry, (Ephesians 4:12),**
- **That eternal salvation is made possible <u>only</u> through the redemptive work of Jesus Christ on Calvary, And that the eternal God has purposely planted (me/us) in _____ (define community) to be a lighthouse to those without Him.**

We (I) hereby commit on this _____ day of _____ in the year of our Lord _____, to assume our (my) responsibilities to reach this community of which we are (I am) a part, and through the building of relationships with those outside the community of faith, seek to bring the message of eternal life available "by grace, through faith" in the completed work of our Lord and Savior, Jesus Christ.

In making this commitment before God and the witness of another, we (I) seek to reach out to our (my) community, to fulfill this Scriptural mandate, and give all glory to God for what He might choose by His grace to accomplish through our (my) efforts.

_____

_____

Authorized Signatures

_____

In Witness Thereof

(Over)

111

Name of organization _____

Address _____

City _____ State _____ Zip _____

Country _____

Telephone _____

Fax _____

E-Mail _____

(Signatures should reflect the name and position of two church (or organization) leaders. Underneath each signature, please type or print the name. Upon completion, please mail a copy of this covenant to: *Transforming Culture Ministries*, 6830 Fox Lake N. Drive, Indianapolis, IN 46278 USA)